ELEMENTS
OF *family*
STYLE

ELEMENTS OF *family* STYLE

ELEGANT SPACES *for* EVERYDAY LIFE

ERIN GATES

ATRIA BOOKS

New York London Toronto Sydney New Delhi

ATRIA BOOKS

AN IMPRINT OF SIMON & SCHUSTER, INC.

1230 Avenue of the Americas

New York, NY 10020

First Atria Books hardcover edition April 2019

ATRIA BOOKS and colophon are registered trademarks of
Simon & Schuster, Inc.

For information about special discounts for bulk purchases, please
contact Simon & Schuster Special Sales at 1-866-506-1949 or
business@simonandschuster.com.

The Simon & Schuster Speakers Bureau can bring authors to your
live event. For more information, or to book an event, contact the
Simon & Schuster Speakers Bureau at 866-248-3049 or visit our
website at www.simonspeakers.com.

Interior design by JENNIFER K. BEAL DAVIS
Jacket design by JENNIFER K. BEAL DAVIS
Jacket art by Michael J. Lee (cover), Sarah Mason Walden for Peacoquette
Designs (spine), and Thom Filicia for Kravet (back cover)

Manufactured in the United States of America

1 3 5 7 9 10 8 6 4 2

Library of Congress Cataloging-in-Publication Data has been applied for.

ISBN 978-1-5011-3730-3

ISBN 978-1-5011-3731-0 (ebook)

ALSO BY ERIN GATES: *ELEMENTS OF STYLE*

For Henry, my sunshine,
my only sunshine.

CONTENTS

INTRODUCTION

Since the publication of my first book, *Elements of Style: Designing a Home & a Life,* in 2014, a lot has changed in my world. My business has grown to include more clients from across the country. I launched my own line of rugs and home accessories. My husband, Andrew, and I completed two additions on our home. And of course, the biggest change of all: we finally had a baby!

If you follow me on my blog or other social media channels, you are well aware of my son Henry's existence—I've pretty much documented every move he's made and outfit he's worn since his birth. It's possible that if he had his own Instagram account he'd have far more followers than I do.

OPPOSITE: Creating spaces for "adults only" time is important, too—like in this living room we designed with a sculptural mantel surrounding a cozy gas fireplace.

While I have to admit that even though the tiny jeans and miniature sneakers are positively adorable and fun to photograph, the added bonus of having Henry in my life is that he's made me a better, more thoughtful designer. I've always thought of my own home as my laboratory where I can try out ideas and fabrics and furniture in private, on my own dime. I don't like to experiment too much when my client is writing the checks! Finding out that a certain fabric does NOT repel chocolate chip cookie stains made by sticky little hands is a discovery I'd prefer to make myself.

These days, whenever I'm designing spaces for people who have a baby or are expecting, I can speak knowledgeably and with confidence about what is a smart choice and what is something they may regret or need to get rid of as the baby grows from immobile infant to fearless toddler and beyond. And when it comes to older kids, I have an ever-expanding arsenal of lovely but tough-as-nails textiles and finishes that can stand up to their shenanigans, as well as a long list of tried-and-true tips for keeping family spaces tidy and chic.

Here's the best part: making child-friendly choices doesn't mean that you need to give up on having a stylish home. In fact, most of the homes I showcased in my last book WERE designed for families with children. The assumption that "we have kids now, so we need to hide all of the nice pieces and cover our sofa in plastic" is not true! Sure, you don't want to upholster your sofa in silk, but honestly, who would? I'm far messier than Henry in many regards (I'm looking at you, red wine stains on my rug), and our two dogs get the blame for messing up a duvet cover or six . . . so we can't blame it all on Henry.

However, you do need to make concessions and plan ahead when living with littles. From finding a place to store the 1,568,345 Lego pieces strewn across the living room floor to seeking out dining chairs that are easy to wipe up after a spill, there are some things that you do have to think carefully about or change when your family grows. Luckily for us all, the marketplace has responded to these needs in a big way, and there are far more fashionable choices that are also durable and easy to care for than there were even just a few years ago.

That said, I also want to teach Henry to respect his surroundings, including our home. We live in a society that seems to defer to children and cater to their every whim and I don't think that is necessarily healthy or appropriate. It's okay to tell Junior that no, he can't eat his peanut butter and jelly in your bed or use water guns in the house. My hope is that by establishing sensible boundaries and sticking to rules that apply within the home, Henry will develop a greater sense of responsibility

for the world at large, and I think that can only foster a heathier respect toward adults. No matter how much we want to give our kids everything (and avoid meltdowns), I believe it's crucial for them to understand that they can't have everything.

By far the most important thing I've learned through designing homes for dozens of loving families and my own is that a house is only a home when it's filled with the people you love. No place will feel as special as the one that's full of laughter and love. I've also discovered

that even the most pristine, swoonworthy spaces won't be fun to live *with* if you can't live *in* them. Like our families, our homes are always evolving and must be adaptable and functional as well as beautiful. That's what makes life interesting and pleasurable.

I hope this book inspires you to create the kind of home that you can feel not only proud of but also comfortable in, surrounded by the people who light up your world.

—ERIN GATES, 2019

FAMILY SPACES

the "non-diy" family

I was thirty-five when I found out I was pregnant with Henry. By that time, most of my close friends already had four- or five-year-olds plus an infant or one on the way. I'd waited to start my family because, for a long time, I was not sure if I wanted to be a parent. My doctor had gently brought up the fact that a woman's fertility declines in her midthirties, but for a long time I felt like, "Wait, this feels like something I should be a thousand percent sure of before I do it, right?" Creating a life was not something to take lightly or do just because the clock was ticking. So, I waited.

OPPOSITE: This vignette perfectly illustrates how I like décor to reflect someone's life story: the table is an antique from my parents, the blue chinoiserie pot has some of the ashes from my first dog, the picture is from our engagement, and the book underneath was written by my father-in-law.

And then it happened: I woke up one day and knew in my heart that I really wanted to be a mom. It was like an alarm bell went off. I looked around at all I had accomplished with my career—I'd written my first book and was well on my way to even greater success both personally and professionally—and felt ready. That sense of gratification was what I thought I needed to spur my ovaries to get prepared to procreate. It was time to get in the game.

Or not, as Andrew and I soon found out.

After a year of trying and failing to get pregnant, we went in search of professional help and answers. Luckily, where we live there is no shortage of doctors specializing in this field and fertility treatment was covered by our insurance (a benefit not granted to many people, which enrages me). After a barrage of tests, tons of poking and prodding, and some rather embarrassing feats on my husband's part, we were diagnosed with "unexplained fertility issues." If there is anything more aggravating than hearing, "Well, we know you can't get pregnant easily but we don't know why," I don't know what it is. Their best guess was that for one reason or another, my eggs were wonky more often than not, so my chances of getting pregnant in any given month were much lower than most women's. Having Andrew's "swimmers" graded as "Michael Phelps level" didn't

help with my guilt and self-blame. He, however, wanted to have T-shirts made declaring his prowess.

After several failed attempts to get pregnant through less invasive interventions (Clomid, intrauterine insemination . . .), we went all in with in vitro fertilization, "given my age and all" (cue angriest emoji ever). As anxious as I was about going through the retrieval process, I was super hopeful that if I did all this work, it would certainly result in a baby. How could it not?

Spoiler alert: IVF usually doesn't work on the first try. The first cycle of IVF is like throwing a dart with your eyes closed. They use the standard dosages and medicines and see how your body reacts. More often than not, it takes more than one cycle to get the formula right. We knew that going in. Still, I will never forget the despair I felt after finding out our transfer did not take—and that not one of the remaining fourteen embryos was healthy enough to freeze. I thought for sure at least a handful would pass muster and that I wouldn't have to go through the torturous process of egg harvesting again for a very long time.

I remember sitting in my car, phone in my hand, ugly-crying Claire Danes style, trying to gather myself enough to go into my office and face the day. Business doesn't pause when you are going through medical treatment, no matter how emotional you might be. In some ways, work can be a good distraction; it keeps you engaged in the world. But some days you want to just pull the covers up over your head and hide, alone with all the fears and disappointment swirling and swelling in your brain.

Fortunately, throughout all of this, I had not only Andrew and my friends and family but also my loyal blog readers by my side. I'm so thankful that I had such a strong online community to whom I could vent, at least virtually. As you may know, I have very little filter when it comes to sharing details of my personal life! By letting it all out in the open on my blog, not only did I feel so much less alone, but I was also convinced to switch doctors and try a different clinic. Four readers had recommended one particular specialist in my neighborhood, and I immediately made an appointment with her. I had not connected on a personal level with my last doctor and felt very much like a cog in a giant machine at the hospital with which she was affiliated. When I met with this new doctor, I knew I'd found The One. She gave me answers, a sense of real hope—and her direct email address. Score!!! Because of her, I felt ready to face another round of drugs and surgery.

And man, did that personal touch make a difference. Of course, there were tweaks to my medications, and I did participate in acupuncture this time around, but I do believe that my positive attitude and the comfort I felt with my new doctor were real game changers. During this cycle we ended up with a near-perfect embryo to transfer, plus three more to freeze. When I got the news, I wept tears of gratitude. I had never thought getting pregnant would take so much work and will and spirit, but apparently, this was how I was meant to create my family. I now know SO many other women who have had to go this route—if you're going through it now, please know you're not alone.

We transferred our one perfect embryo and while I was hopeful, I knew there were more to try so I wasn't as petrified as I was the first time. And then, two weeks later, there were two lines on the pregnancy test. I could barely comprehend it. I blinked and looked again; I didn't trust my own eyes. Again, there it was. Positive. I was pregnant. I took five or six more tests just for the fun of seeing it turn positive.

But after what I'd been through I didn't fully believe the test, and I didn't trust my body to do what it was supposed to do. My body had failed me so many times already. So, Andrew and I were cautiously overjoyed. Eventually we were able to let go of our fear and not only enjoy the news but also share it with others (although our favorite Starbucks barista became suspicious early on, when I started ordering half-caf coffees!). I have never been so excited to write a blog post in my entire career. I titled it "The Post I've Waited Years to Write" and I wasn't disappointed in the least by the reaction it got. My readers seemed as excited as I was, and in a way it was like the best surprise party ever with thousands of friends all in one room. It was one of the happiest days of my life.

Of course, I was thrilled to design the baby's nursery. We found out the gender at twelve weeks—the only bonus to being a "grandma pregnancy," due to my age—and I went ALL OUT with plans for a space for my little boy. Since it took so much work to get pregnant with him, I knew a second pregnancy was far from certain. This could be my one shot at designing my ultimate fantasy nursery. From a custom mural wallpaper to designer crib and changer, I had an extraordinary time planning this special space. I actually came up with two completely different schemes and was torn between them for weeks. One was bold, employing a navy and orange scheme with more graphic touches, and the other was softer, with a painted light-gray mural and the palest blue. I was down to the wire on picking one when I realized that

I'd get to do a big-boy room someday, but I might never get to do a baby nursery again. In the end I went with the calmer palette, which ended up being perfect for a newborn. It gave me such a feeling of peace to work on this space (that is, when I wasn't facedown in a toilet bowl swearing I would never, *EVER* do this again!).

I can't lie: I had a tough pregnancy and battled morning sickness until roughly twenty-six weeks. The all-day nausea was so uncomfortable that there were moments I wondered just WHY I wanted this so desperately. So, for me, the third trimester was the best by far. I could keep food down and felt comfortable in my body and with the fact that the pregnancy was no longer in jeopardy. I could breathe a sigh of relief and enjoy! Before I knew it, I was Instagramming from the hospital during a long but ultimately calm and easy delivery (a big thank-you to the genius behind the epidural and all related drugs!).

I still have to catch my breath when I look at Henry. I can't believe this perfect, sweet, adorable boy who loves to drive tractors around the backyard and asks me to rub his back before he goes to bed each night is my son. Mine. The same little person who would kick my sciatic nerve and cause weeks of nausea worse than seasickness. The same one who would press his little foot up against my belly like something out of *Alien* and freak me out. It's so surreal. Someday he'll know how hard we fought to bring him into this world, and how very much he was and is loved, wanted, and cherished from the moment he was an eight-cell embryo until today and forever. Despite all the cool accomplishments and projects I've completed, he is, by far, the best work I have ever produced.

Our journey to create our family isn't over. Well, it might be—but not without a fight. Around Henry's first birthday, we decided we wanted to go for a second baby. The process has been far more brutal than our first attempt to conceive. In a little over a year I have suffered three pregnancy losses, all of which have left me gutted and more exhausted than I've ever been in my life. Not only from the emotional turbulence of the losses themselves, but the draining fertility process that comes BEFORE the bad news. The drugs and needles, the intense exams and tests—couple that with chasing after a toddler and a full-time job and it's enough to send even the sanest gal to the looney bin. We haven't given up—we'll keep trying until we feel it's time to stop.

Henry is wonderfully oblivious to the stress we've felt trying to give him a sibling. I hide my tears and Andrew steps in with extra hugs and snuggles when I need time to collapse and grieve. Always, we bounce back, that little Henry smile and those sparkly eyes lifting me from the depths every time. I can't be sad for long with this magical boy doing silly dances and singing the *PAW Patrol* theme song to himself as he falls asleep. I know how lucky I am to have someone who calls out "Mommy!" in the middle of the night and asks me to kiss his boo-boos. It can be hard to conjure gratitude for all I do have when I'm focused on what I do not, but as a wise friend once said to me, feeling and exhibiting gratitude is the best way to pray. I fully believe in this and try to practice small acts of gratitude every single day.

FAMILY ROOMS

Whether your family room is part of an open-concept floor plan connected to the kitchen or in a space by itself, this area of the home is one of the most used and probably the most visible to family and friends, especially those with kids. The days of formal entertaining seem to be over, so more likely than not, even if you have a formal living room, you and your guests will end up in the family room.

The keys to creating a space that functions well, looks great, and stands up to the wear and tear of small children and pets are rather simple: tons of attractive storage options to hide clutter; big, well-made comfy seating; and a large coffee table or ottoman on which to kick up your feet, play a board game, eat dinner (come on, we all do it), or enjoy a cocktail. And of course, a TV (which we'll address later).

OPPOSITE: Our new family room doesn't have a big footprint, but the vaulted ceiling makes it feel large and bright.

For the final renovation of our current home, we tore down our sunroom and rebuilt it as a family room, which has been one of the best decisions we've made with our house. We spend SO much time in this bright, happy room with Henry . . . and without! I wanted it to feel open and filled with light, so we decided to vault the ceiling, which makes the modest square footage seem much larger than it is, and incorporate as many windows as we could. The rest of our house has low ceilings and is a little on the dark side, so this room feels like a breath of fresh air. I kept furniture to a minimum knowing I'd want Henry to have space to play, but I was sure to provide ample seating for us to hang out as a family and watch *The Lion King* for the three hundredth time or a different movie once Andrew and I are alone. It's worked out beautifully.

The family room is the spot where you should purchase the highest-quality seating you can afford. Be it a sectional or a couch, this piece (or pieces) will get a great deal of use, so they need to be comfortable but also really durable. There's nothing worse than spending a lot of money on a sofa only to have all the cushions sag and fall flat after six months of wear. I myself have made this mistake! A well-made, sturdily constructed piece will last for many years to come, so as I advise my clients, when looking at pricing and quality, always err on the side of the old adage "It's better to cry once than twice."

ABOVE: I have found natural cowhide to be one of the most durable materials on the planet—I've cleaned red wine, ice cream, and chocolate off this ottoman!

OPPOSITE: The see-through fireplace was a big investment but one that helps connect the family room to the living room. And the skinny built-in makes use of every inch!

BEST PIECE OF ADVICE YOU GIVE TO CLIENTS WHO HAVE KIDS?
My priorities have always been people, then pets, then things.

—NATE BERKUS
INTERIOR DESIGNER AND AUTHOR

WHAT TO LOOK FOR IN A LONG-TERM UPHOLSTERY PIECE

- A KILN-DRIED HARDWOOD FRAME: The frame is the skeleton of the piece, so you want it to be made of sturdy wood that won't warp. A good test—lift one front corner of the sofa a few inches; if the other front leg doesn't rise to the same height as the one you are lifting, it's not a sturdy frame.

- QUALITY JOINT CONSTRUCTION: Make sure the joints aren't glued or stapled but rather connected by mortise-and-tenon, dowel, or tongue-and-groove joints.

- SPRING-DOWN SEAT CUSHIONS: Constructed much like a mattress, this type of cushion won't sag and will be nice and supportive, yet soft. Firmly filled down back cushions will also sag less and need less fluffing.

- HIGHLY DURABLE FABRIC: There are so many great options these days for family-friendly, pet-proof upholstery. Indoor/outdoor fabrics that still feel nice and stain-resistant/treated fabrics are great options. Be sure to check the durability rating of the fabric being used—sometimes things that feel sturdy turn out not to be rated as such. The two standards by which durability is measured in the fabric industry are the Wyzenbeek and Martindale methods, which involve machines rubbing fabric to see how long it takes to break down. For high-traffic pieces, like sofas, we like to use "heavy use"-rated fabrics, while drapes and pillows can be "light use."

MARTINDALE

Light use: 6,000–9,000 cycles

Medium use: 9,000–20,000 cycles

Heavy use: 20,000+ cycles

WYZENBEEK

Light use: 6,000–9,000 double rubs

Medium use: 9,000–15,000 double rubs

Heavy use: 15,000+ double rubs

- SLIPCOVERED OPTIONS: Having a slipcover is a great option as you can remove it and have it dry-cleaned or laundered instead of needing to reupholster a piece or live with icky stains. Look for a slipcover that is fitted tight to the frame to avoid it looking disheveled or sloppy. Also, never tumble dry a slipcover, as it will shrink! Hang it to dry, but put it on when still very slightly damp so it molds back to the piece.

OPPOSITE: We chose a sturdy hardwood-framed sectional done in an outdoor fabric for this family's busy living area.

This open family room combines wonderful grown-up features like the rug and custom pillows with the focus still being on family (you can totally work in a teepee!).

LEFT: I absolutely love this combination of red and blue—it feels fresh and not stuffy or old-fashioned. The sectional is done in an outdoor fabric for durability; however, it looks like any other woven material.

OPPOSITE: In this built-in we used a fantastic patterned grass cloth, which adds a special level of detail not always seen in most homes. The items on the shelf really pop against the material.

SECTIONAL BUYING TIP

The terminology can be confusing when trying to decide whether what you need is a "left-hand facing" chaise or "right-hand facing." When facing the sofa in your space (NOT sitting ON the sofa), if you want the chaise on the right side, it's "right-hand facing." If you want it on the left, it's "left-hand facing." This gets mixed up often and it's a huge bummer when your sofa arrives in the wrong configuration, so triple-check with your vendor when ordering, as they make mistakes too—it's happened to me!

STYLISH SECTIONALS

CLASSIC & COZY

A higher shelter arm keeps you feeling cozy, while the split cushions keep things from getting saggy. This is a style that goes with any type of décor.

TIGHT BACK & TUFTED

In leather or fabric, this style is sleek, streamlined, and almost impossible to dishevel. No back cushions mean no fuss! The high arm means you have to be mindful of the height of your side tables—look for tables 3–4 inches lower than the arm.

TAILORED SLIPCOVER

Slipcovers can look sloppy if too loose, but a tailored version is a great marriage between cleanability and style. Note if the fabric being used is washable or dry-clean only before laundering.

STREAMLINED BASE

If you like a hint of wood but want a more modern option than something with a traditional turned leg, this is your style! A great transitional style that works with both contemporary and traditional décor.

"Sectionals" used to be a word associated with ugly and out-of-date interiors. No longer! The sectional is the most efficient way to offer lots of seating in a family space, and with so many different kinds available, you won't be compromising on your style one bit. From streamlined and modern to classic roll arms or a washable slipcover, there is a sectional for every home out there!

TRADITIONAL ROLL ARM

Timeless and classically beautiful, this style of sofa or sectional will never look dated. The lower arm is comfy for napping and the legs add an element of detail.

CHESTERFIELD

Handsome and sturdy, the Chesterfield sectional is another tough-as-nails style (especially in leather), with no fussiness about it and stately good looks.

MODERN BENCH SEAT

The single bench seat is a great look that makes a sofa appear less busy and a little more modern. Make sure the cushion is very well made or it may sag in the middle over time.

CONTEMPORARY

Yes, you CAN have a modern, cool-looking sectional! Angled arms, metal or wood bases, and tufting all make for a unique and shapely staple for your family room.

This kind of open, sunny space is ideal for families—we kept it neutral overall with accents of blues spread throughout in smaller doses, leaving it open to change in the future.

DURABLE FABRICS CHEAT SHEET

- WHITE DUCK/DENIM: Truly the only way you can have a white sofa AND dogs/kids/red wine. This thick fabric is bleachable and great for slip-covered items.

- SOLUTION-DYED ACRYLIC: This is outdoor fabric like Sunbrella. The material comes in a variety of formats—from linen-like weaves to plush velvets! Some can even be cleaned with bleach.

- VELVET: Avoid silk or 100 percent cotton velvet as they can stain and show wear easily. Polyester-blend versions can be super durable and stain resistant. They also make outdoor-grade velvet now!

- STAIN-RESISTANT FINISHES: Some fabrics now come with stain-resistant finishes already applied (brands like Crypton). These can be easier to clean than other linens or wovens, but test a sample to be sure, as they are not bulletproof!

- ULTRASUEDE: This was one of the first fabrics marketed as kid/stain-proof. It's not my personal favorite. I don't like how you can see finger marks and swirls, but it does wear like iron on high-traffic furniture.

- LEATHER: Leather furniture is incredibly durable. Although it's not the coziest for snuggling on during movie night, it is fantastic for otto-man-style cocktail tables. Just test the leather for scratchability before buying as some are more prone to it than others (be especially careful if you have pets, as claw marks are a big drag!). Liquids and grease may stain, but there are ways to gently clean and improve the look of such stains.

- FAUX LEATHER/VINYL: It may sound terrible and make you think of the material used in diners, but faux leather has come SUCH a long way. I love using it on banquettes and counter stools as it's virtually indestructible and comes in great colors.

- CONTRACT-GRADE FABRICS: These are made for places like hotels and restaurants, so they are incredibly durable; however, patterns and textures are limited and most are only available to the trade.

OPPOSITE: In this family room we went bold with a custom chair done in a really fun wide stripe. Simple woven wood shades dress up a large window.

BEST PIECE OF ADVICE YOU GIVE TO CLIENTS WHO HAVE KIDS?
Invest in amazing pieces that you can reupholster numerous times. If you have a piece of furniture that is in good shape and good quality, it will stand the test of time (and kids!).

—SUYSEL DEPEDRO CUNNINGHAM &
ANNE MAXWELL FOSTER
TILTON FENWICK

CORRALLING
THE CLUTTER

If there is one universal truth to raising a family, it's that there is SO. MUCH. STUFF. From Lego parts to baby dolls and everything in between, there are piles and piles of toys and what I call "small bits" that kids are apt to leave all over the floor. So I always advise creating the most storage possible in the family room (and other rooms too, as there is always overflow!). There is no need for storage to look juvenile or clash with the "style" of your home, though. We utilize various types of furniture to make storage that blends in with the rest of the design.

BEST TIP FOR ORGANIZING?
Store things low enough so that the kids can put it all away without your help. We do this for their clothes, toys, etc. We even keep our dinnerware and glassware in drawers in the kitchen so the kids can empty the dishwasher.

—LAUREN LIESS
LAUREN LIESS & CO.

OPPOSITE: In this built-in we used a fun faux wood wallpaper to give texture to the back wall, which gives depth to the unit.

BUILT-INS: Customized built-ins ARE pricey, but in most cases so very much worth it! They maximize every inch of storage (horizontally AND vertically). If you feel open shelving will just invite more clutter, cover the shelves with doors. Contact a local carpenter to help you with a layout and design if you don't work with an interior designer.

BOOKCASES: Always an asset in a room, bookcases are a great way to add height to a space. Whether you use simple shelves to display pictures and store favorite reads or cubby-style shelves you can load up with cute bins or baskets to keep all the toys and small bits organized, bookcases are a must when you have kids. Use a nice tall pair flanking a media console for a "faux built-in" look.

STORAGE OTTOMANS/TABLES: Make your furniture work double time! An ottoman that also serves as storage is a wonderful use of space, especially in smaller homes. Add a tray for drinks, magazines, and remotes and keep blankets, board games, or toys inside. Always think about how to sneak in extra storage. If you need a bench or have your eye on a pair of cube ottomans, look for models that have storage inside!

BASKETS & BINS: I can't think of a family room I've designed that doesn't have a basket or six somewhere in the room! Baskets, especially those with lids, are such a great place to dump small bits. Yes, we all do it—just grab an armload of beeping and talking toys, stuff them in, and put on the lid. TA DA! Instant organization. I like to buy matching sets to keep everything looking coordinated and crisp.

OPPOSITE: A large abstract piece of art (from a catalog store, believe it or not) adds drama and a modern touch to the otherwise transitional design.

TV

Luckily, technology is keeping pace with our design desires and need for giant TVs everywhere in the home. There are framed TVs that turn to art when off and even TVs that will display whatever pattern is on your wall to camouflage themselves into the décor! But you don't necessarily need to spring for a fancy new TV. Built-ins frame out a flat-screen nicely, as do media bookcase systems—they make the TV feel like less of a glaringly obvious focal point. If you hang your TV on the wall, consider installing a gallery of art or photos around it to trick the eye. Wherever and however it's placed in the room, don't worry too much—like elbows, we all have them; no need to go to great lengths to hide them!

RIGHT: In this large open family room we dressed up the built-in with grass cloth and used an ottoman in a faux leather in place of a coffee table. A swivel chair allows for TV viewing and conversation.

HOW TO MIX PATTERNS

One of the questions I get most often from blog readers is, "How do I mix patterns properly?" A lot of it comes down to your personal taste. Are you more of a sleek minimalist or do lots of patterns and details make you happy?

There is a formula we like to use when pulling together a whole room, or just choosing throw pillows, that can make mixing patterns a little easier.

- BRING TOGETHER DIFFERENT SCALES: If you use too many patterns of the same scale, your space will look incredibly busy. Use a larger pattern, a medium-size one, a small one, and then a solid or two.
- MIX UP THE TYPES OF PATTERN: We like to think of it this way— an organic pattern (i.e., floral, botanical, or paisley), which is usually the larger scale, a geometric or stripe (typically a medium scale), and a small scale (a good example is a tiny diamond weave or dot).
- ADD TEXTURE: I always like to incorporate different textures to add visual interest and dimension—velvets, printed patterns, and wovens being my most-often-used combinations. Be sure to mix it up, as using only one type of texture can look flat and boring.

OPPOSITE: Pairing pillows and patterns can be tricky, but typically we like to mix a solid (with a border or without) with a geometric pattern as well as a more organic, free-form pattern.

In this living room we added pops of bright yellow to bring in some attitude while maintaining the modern-meets-traditional aesthetic. The walls are painted in Benjamin Moore Balboa Mist at 50 percent strength.

RUGS FOR HIGH-TRAFFIC AREAS

Rugs are one of the first things people with kids ask me about when designing a family space, with their concern being durability AND comfort. With kids playing on the floor and lots of bare feet, you want something that feels nice, of course, but also something pretty to look at that doesn't stain easily. And hey, that translates to grown-ups too: I've been known to spill a full glass of red wine all over my rug on (multiple) occasions. We've had lots of experience with various types of rugs, and here are our recommendations.

GREEN LIGHT

SYNTHETIC FIBERS: A synthetic carpet or rug (nylon, olefin, etc.), whether wall to wall or an area rug, is the best choice for active families (including animals) where pet, food, and beverage accidents will routinely occur. Patterns and medium tones will do best at concealing stains.

TOUGHEST "LIVING WITH KIDS" DECORATING LESSON?
No matter how hard you say you won't, you WILL have some hideous exersaucer or swing in your living room! Embrace it. Keep the hideous stuff to a minimum, but accept that it will happen.

—SUYSEL DEPEDRO CUNNINGHAM & ANNE MAXWELL FOSTER
TILTON FENWICK

OPPOSITE: This sunroom also acts as a family space. We kept the original wicker furniture and updated the cushions in new outdoor fabrics—combining buffalo checks, solid with piping, and botanical prints. The rug is also indoor/outdoor!

100 PERCENT WOOL RUGS: Wool wall-to-wall carpet and area rugs are best in high and regular foot-traffic areas such as stairs, hallways, bedrooms, living rooms, and dining rooms. The reason is that wool hides soil behind its cuticles very well. General soil from foot/shoe traffic or the stray bunch of crumbs usually cleans up well, but don't wait until it looks dirty or it may get too deep into the fibers. Patterns (like my leopard runner) are excellent for hiding dirt!

PERSIAN/ORIENTAL RUGS: These rugs are usually wool or a combination of wool and silk. The popular vintage or distressed wool, low-to-no-pile versions are quite durable and hide dirt and stains well. These types are great for kitchens, entries, and layered over larger jute or sisal rugs. Finer rugs that are made with silk should be treated with more care and used in less heavily trafficked areas of the home.

ABOVE: Dogs can be just as messy as kids, which is why we chose durable fabrics and rugs for this home that contains both! The TV is concealed behind the doors above the fireplace.

OPPOSITE: Canary-yellow pillows sing on this sofa—a great example of how small doses of color can really amp up a space.

PROCEED WITH CAUTION

JUTE/SISAL: These materials are made from natural plant fibers that usually withstand foot traffic; however, these floor coverings do not usually do well with noticeable soil, pet, food, or beverage stains as they are virtually impossible to clean successfully. They also adversely react to wet-cleaning and can buckle when saturated with water.

TREAD LIGHTLY

SILK/WOOL-SILK COMBO: While silk and wool-silk combination rugs can be professionally cleaned, it's usually best to clean the whole carpet or rug

ABOVE: This family room is a bright twist on traditional décor with tones of blue and green mixing together through lots of fun patterns grounded by a natural jute-and-wool rug.

when an accident occurs. Sometimes cleaning just a spot on these materials can result in a lightened or brightened section that tends to stand out. If the whole piece is cleaned, any change in tone will be uniform throughout. Bamboo silk rugs are a problem to wet-clean as they flatten and become distorted.

VISCOSE/RAYON/TENCEL: These materials contain wood pulp, and floor coverings with these materials do not do well with high foot traffic or food/pet stains. These materials do not like water. They often take on a permanent distorted or matted appearance when wet-cleaning is attempted and take a very long time to dry. I had one of these rugs and it was IMPOSSIBLE with my dogs!

ABOVE: A traditional rug serves as a jumping-off point for the palette of this family room by California designer Jenn Feldman, but the modern lines of the rest of the furniture keep it from feeling stuffy and dated—a great combination of styles.

WHEN SPOTS & SPILLS DO HAPPEN...

Spills and stains are inevitable when living with kids. It's part of the fun—just embrace it! You can have as many "no raspberries in the living room" rules as you want, but accidents will happen. And some nonaccidents too, like when a certain child, who shall remain nameless, thinks it's super fun to stomp Goldfish and blueberries into the carpet. And while you may have used durable fabrics and rugs all over the house, you may still need to attack those stains with all the firepower in your arsenal.

1. TREAT AHEAD OF TIME: Research local companies that come to your house and pre-treat your upholstered pieces, rugs, and drapes with a stain repellent. We recommend this protective step to all our clients.

2. BLOT: Never rub a fresh stain as it will just push it deeper into the fabric and/or make the fabric pill. Use a white cloth to prevent any color transfer. You can use a small amount of dish soap mixed with water to treat, but always test first in an inconspicuous place like the bottom of a cushion.

3. VACUUM: Use the hose attachment to vacuum the area and remove small particles or larger pieces of soil. Also note that a weekly vacuuming of your upholstery helps keep it in its best shape overall.

4. SOAK IT UP: If the area is still wet or the stain is particularly greasy, a wool-safe absorbent powder should be applied covering the affected/stained area. The powder should sit on the affected area for approximately five hours before it is vacuumed up. You can try cornstarch for a natural method.

5. CALL IN THE PROS: Sometimes you just will not be able to get a stain out, and in that case, call a professional cleaner to come treat it. It's cheaper than having to buy new furniture or rugs.

6. BEWARE THE NASTY STUFF: Bodily fluids from kids or pets (urine, vomit, etc.) are stains that are very hard to treat and often leave marks due to the high acid content, which can loosen dyes and fibers in the fabric or rug. These types of stains may be permanent on natural fibers.

Thank you to MWI Fiber-Shield for the professional cleaning tips!

OPPOSITE: A wool rug in a saturated color helps conceal wear and tear as well as spills.

ABOVE: I used outdoor fabric on my sectional slipcover, giving Henry the freedom to eat ice cream while watching *PAW Patrol*.

OPEN CONCEPT

We hear it all the time on our favorite home renovation shows: everyone wants "open-concept" living spaces. There is a reason for this—it's easier to multitask if you can watch your kids playing while also making dinner or paying bills at the kitchen counter. The downside, however, is that you can see *everything*, all the time. Your kids' toys mingle with your dining area and their snacks creep their way into the living area. So be sure to offer up lots of places to store things and try to make each area of the space dedicated to a specific purpose.

OPPOSITE: Designer Kate Coughlin did a tremendous job unifying this large, open-concept family room and making it feel cozy through swaths of bright color.

ABOVE, LEFT TO RIGHT: The casual dining area of this Kate Coughlin-designed space features tough-as-nails bistro chairs but also a show-stopping light fixture. ❘ Another great example of spreading color throughout a room, even in unexpected places.

This massively airy and open family room in the country is one of my all-time favorites! Patterned drapes emphasize the ceiling height while a textured rug grounds the cozy furniture.

CLOCKWISE, FROM TOP LEFT: A pair of leather ottomans add optional seating, while the modern painting is an unexpected touch against the stone chimney. I A small café table floating between the family room and kitchen area gives the family a spot to play a game or have a snack. I When designing a room that is open from the kitchen right through to the family room, I like to keep the décor unified as much as possible and treat it like one big room instead of three separate spaces.

SPLURGE VS. SAVE: FAMILY ROOM

SPLURGE: SECTIONAL OR SOFA—As mentioned earlier, this is the most important piece to buy the best quality you can afford.

SAVE: ACCENT SEATING OR POUFS—These items do not need to be as well-made and can come from discount stores or vintage shops!

SPLURGE: COFFEE TABLE OR COCKTAIL OTTOMAN—This piece will get a ton of use in a busy family room, so buy something made of solid material that can withstand a beating (or years of board games!). Real wood, leather upholstery, or stone tops will be your best bet. Something with a lower shelf for keeping clutter out of sight is also a big bonus.

SAVE: ACCENT TABLES—These pieces needn't be expensive; utilize Lucite, metals, resin—anything, really. If holding a lamp they should be weighty enough not to tip over but not so fancy that you're devastated when a drink ring appears.

SPLURGE: DURABLE FABRICS FOR UPHOLSTERY—So many retail vendors now offer indoor/outdoor or treated fabrics, so look into all the options available. Ask for samples to take home and test them with everything you have—ketchup, berries, wine . . . just go to town! Better to learn though a sample that something isn't as durable as it's marketed to be than to find out after you've made an expensive purchase.

SAVE: PILLOWS & RUGS—These are items you can really save on, as you may want to swap them out as your tastes change (or your family changes!). There are so many great options out there—just make sure the pillows have a nice filler (down, unless you or your children are allergic) so that

WHAT CLICHÉ/OUTDATED ADVICE DO YOU WISH PEOPLE WOULD STOP LISTENING TO WHEN IT COMES TO DECORATING A FAMILY HOME?

Going dark on every surface isn't the only solution with kids. So many people think they need a dark rug, dark walls, dark sofa, and dark pillows to hide everything. There are many materials out there now that make it easy to go light in color with easy cleanup.

—SHEA MCGEE
STUDIO MCGEE

they look more expensive than they are. Flat-weave wool or indoor/outdoor rugs are durable and typically quite affordable; I have a great one from IKEA in my basement that looks like a million bucks!

OPPOSITE: In a downtown Boston condo, we used the same fabric for pillows on the sofa and the host chairs at the dining table as a way to connect the two spaces.

ABOVE, LEFT TO RIGHT: A modern gas fireplace feature divides the living space from dining in this condo and creates a fabulous nook by the kitchen for a cocktail. ❙ A pair of pretty tufted sofas topped with pillows in soft tones always look elegant and refined.

ABOVE, LEFT TO RIGHT: The two-toned blue grass cloth and bevy of blue decorative accents reflect the beach, a favorite vacation spot for these clients. **I** Emily Butler designed this navy built-in to not only optimize storage but also to conceal the TV without covering it up. The library sconces are a perfect touch.

SPLURGE: BUILT-INS—There is no better way to organize a room than a smart built-in. With custom shelving to keep books, pictures, and other smaller objects out of the reach of busy little hands, and drawers in which to hide toys and games, nothing gives you more bang for your buck than a built-in.

SAVE: WALL ART—While original art is a wonderful thing to display in a home, it's not a possibility for many people. There are so many great sources, both online and at brick-and-mortar stores, for reproduction art that there is no need to fret. Consider scale and use large-format art for bigger walls, or use a gallery-style installation for a collection of pictures or prints.

ABOVE: We dressed up a built-in seating area in this window nook in a client's kitchen for the kids to hang out in and display their art and books. Cabinets under the seat and bookshelves flanking it provide ample storage.

SPLURGE: RECESSED LIGHTING—Good lighting makes a space feel so much more open, lively, and welcoming. Installing recessed lighting is an important way to accomplish that task without cluttering a room with accent lamps. I have never once regretting installing it but have kicked myself when I haven't.

ABOVE: Designer Colleen Simonds utilized a whole wall for built-ins to house books in this New York apartment's open-concept living area.

SAVE: TABLE & FLOOR LAMPS—Given the plethora of sources for lighting on the cheap, you can really create nice designer moments in a space without spending a fortune. If feeling adventurous, find an Etsy vendor to make you some custom patterned shades to amp up the look.

ABOVE: Creating a space that is open and yet warm and inviting is essential for young families. This furniture layout, designed by Colleen Simonds, allows for space to play and relax.

When you have unique features in a space, like these beams in this apartment designed by Colleen Simonds, you should let those be the star. Simple cabinetry and décor really show off the texture of the beams in the best way!

KITCHENS & CASUAL DINING

The kitchen is the heart of the home, and it becomes even more so when you add children into the mix. Henry always seems to need a snack. Making sure your kitchen not only functions well but also makes you happy is crucially important, since you'll be spending a good chunk of time in there (as a mom I can tell you I spend way more quality time in the kitchen than I used to before Henry). Now, we all can't have brand-new dream kitchens, but that doesn't mean there aren't easy tweaks you can make to enhance the look and practicality of what you have.

Growing up, we *always*—every night as I recall—had a lovely family dinner cooked by my mom. Cell phones weren't a thing then, so there

OPPOSITE: We did a mini update to our kitchen by swapping in new pendants and barstools and adding a pretty decorative roman valance above the window. Now it feels "finished"!

were no distractions beyond my brother kicking me under the table. I guess you'd likely refer to this as "the good ol' days," with the table set nicely and everyone sitting together and actually talking about their days. My hope is to re-create dinnertimes like this for Henry, but as of right now, dinner in our house is a bit of a screaming hot mess.

Henry, since his newborn days, has not been a "food-motivated" child. He'd much rather be playing, talking, or goofing around than eating. I have to trick or bargain him into eating—and when it's really not going well, I end up caving and giving him his iPad and feeding him myself while he is distracted. It's a terrible practice, I know, but I just want the kid to EAT. Our nanny, Dee, keeps assuring me no child will starve himself to death, but this whole eating thing is a major trigger for my anxiety (as a recovered anorexic, foodcentric issues really push my buttons still!). And I know he KNOWS this: he eats well for Dee every day—he even ate a *plate of calamari* for her—and yet for me he declares pasta with butter "yucky" and only wants ice cream. The little trickster has my number and it's the moment when I feel most defeated as a mom.

So dinnertime consists of me whipping up some chicken nuggets and chopping some veggies and doing a song and dance while Andrew cooks us dinner (yes,

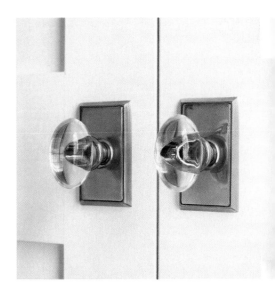

ABOVE: I wanted to make the pantry feel a little special, so I splurged on some beautiful crystal knobs and it made all the difference!

OPPOSITE: When we did our second renovation, we added this invaluable pantry to the mudroom entrance. It's one of the new features I am most grateful for in our house since our kitchen is so small with very little storage.

I'm lucky, I know). When Henry ACTUALLY cleans his plate, it feels like the biggest success of my day, no matter what amazing career goals have been met. Finished writing this book? So what, I GOT MY KID TO EAT HIS DINNER!!!! Now that's something to celebrate. Drinks for everyone!

The other night we all sat down and ate spaghetti together, and I watched in amazement as this little person twirled the noodles around his dinosaur fork and piled bites into his mouth. I got glimpses of this toddler phase ending and us all sitting down together for dinner, like my family did when I was a child, talking about how school was. It was a good reminder that even the stressful parts of motherhood are fleeting—and someday when he's a teenager and taking down a foot-long sub like it's a mere snack, I'll probably wish for just one more moment of when I had to plead to his sweet little face, "*Just one more bite of chicken for Mommy, pleeeeeeeease.*"

RECONSIDER THE LAYOUT

Our former kitchen and dining area was no longer working for our lifestyle (i.e., Henry's indoor scooter hobby), so I reconfigured the furniture layout to allow for more floor space, greater foot-traffic flow, AND comfy seating. By putting a freestanding banquette in the corner we opened up the space and the dining area became a far more comfortable spot in which to dine and hang! And with no contractor involved, it was a pretty painless project. However, if you want to go further or are building a house, built-in banquettes are fantastic for family dining and can offer under-the-seats storage too (great for seasonal or holiday items you don't need to access every day!).

OPPOSITE: Our dining area is now swathed in vinyl grass cloth (kid-proof!) and we swapped our centered dining table and chairs for a custom corner banquette and rectangle pedestal table. The banquette is a combination of outdoor fabric and wipeable vinyl.

SPILL-PROOF SEATING

When picking dining chairs for a casual dining area, I like to choose materials that are easy to wipe, such as faux leather, wood, or acrylic. I've seen even the toughest outdoor fabric meet its demise in a kid-focused dining situation, so if stains drive you crazy or your kids are particularly messy, it's best to leave the upholstered goods for the dining room. This rule also applies to counter stools, except when using faux leather or vinyl, as they wipe up like a dream. We used a vinyl on the seat of our banquette and kept the pretty striped outdoor fabric just for the back—this decision was genius, if I do say so myself!

ABOVE: Proof that high chairs don't have to ruin your dining décor! Henry's white wood chair works seamlessly with our white Windsor chairs.

THE WRITING IS ON THE WALL

Before Henry came along, I redid my kitchen and dining area and installed a beautiful light-gray natural grass cloth on the walls. I dismissed the people who commented that it would get destroyed once I had children and managed to keep it free of red wine and spaghetti sauce stains for two years. A major accomplishment! However, once a child was in the picture, I had to admit, those naysayers were right. The minute Henry could hold a crayon in his hand, he took to scribbling on the walls. And natural grass cloth can't get wet, so cleaning it was not an option. Pretty quickly, I decided I needed to replace it, which I did, with a vinyl grass-cloth paper that looks so much like the real thing that it fools many a visitor! Now I can spray cleaner on it and wipe off whatever mess ends up there, but I still get to enjoy the texture of grass cloth. Vinyl papers are a great option for bathrooms, high-traffic areas, and anywhere kids like to roam.

ABOVE: Since moving the dining area against the wall, we now have a little spot for Henry to have a play table, where he also likes to have his snacks.

ABOVE: We use these durable bistro-style counter stools with woven plastic seats often in kitchens and family dining areas.

LEFT: Designer Julie Richard injects color into this white kitchen with bold red chairs with navy seats and a funky modern light fixture.

OPPOSITE: Designer Alison Sheffield creates this amazingly cozy dining nook off her kitchen with a combination of mid-century and traditional accents.

WHAT CLICHÉ/OUTDATED ADVICE DO YOU WISH PEOPLE WOULD STOP LISTENING TO WHEN IT COMES TO DECORATING A FAMILY HOME?
I wish people would stop telling people to get inexpensive furniture that the "kids can mess up" and then get nicer furniture when they are old enough. Nope.

—LAUREN LIESS
LAUREN LIESS & CO.

LEFT: A peaceful moment in a typically busy kitchen belonging to a family of five.

OPPOSITE: This is one of the most favorite kitchens I've ever done! From the Statuary marble to the fabulous fixtures and custom breakfast table, everything came together beyond beautifully!

UPGRADE YOUR APPLIANCES

A big part of the way your kitchen looks depends on the appliances. Some people prefer to conceal their appliances with cabinetry panels; others make a gorgeous stove the focal point of their entire design (I'm looking at you, fancy French brands!). Just remember this: the most important feature of an appliance is that it is functional. A range that looks jaw-droppingly gorgeous in your space but is tricky to use or doesn't have the features you're comfortable with while cooking is probably not a great choice. However, if you are like me and don't cook, get yourself that beautiful range!

ABOVE: Sometimes plumbing fixtures end up looking like sculptures, like this pot filler.

ABOVE: The barstools here are done in an easy-to-clean outdoor fabric to coordinate with the island paint color and the veining of the marble.

THE COUNTERTOP DEBATE: TO MARBLE OR NOT TO MARBLE

In my last book, I mapped out the qualities of different countertop materials, but it bears revisiting as this is the thing my clients struggle with the most when designing a new kitchen. Everyone loves the look of marble, but not everyone loves the upkeep that comes with it. So here is the advice that I give them when it comes to countertop selection:

MARBLE: If you decide you want the look of real marble, opt for a honed finish (it's slightly more durable) and investigate sealing options with your fabricator. I often advise that people buy an extra-large, attractive wood cutting board they leave out at all times so that they won't be tempted to cut things quickly on the counter. Another option is to do just the island in marble to get the impact of the material, and then do the surrounding perimeter countertops in something durable, like quartz or granite. Another option is to do a backsplash in marble tile and keep the counters a solid quartz or granite, giving you a nice visual of marble without the worry of having it on your workspace.

QUARTZ: Man-made and nearly bulletproof, this material is wonderful for busy families, or those who don't want to deal with any kind of maintenance. The stone patterns available these days are SO realistic, some may not even realize that what you have isn't marble! P.S. I love using the solid white versions in bathrooms when paired with a colored or wood vanity.

LEFT: This kitchen by St. Louis–based designer Jessie Miller stopped me dead in my tracks. Another great example of letting the most unique and textural finishes in your home take front stage!

OPPOSITE: Designer Sarah Scales used so many wonderful materials in this modern but classic kitchen—from the waterfall island to the natural wood cabinets.

LEFT: The finish on these lower cabinets is a wonderful choice to warm up a space with tile floors. The slightly industrial hardware is a unique choice that adds interest.

QUARTZITE: This is one of the most popular options these days for those wanting real stone with natural veining patterns but also increased durability. Each type of quartzite is different, though, so be sure to research and consult with your stone yard about the type you want. While I have had wonderful luck with my vein-cut quartzite, I had a client do the crosscut version of the same stone and it stained horribly. Quartzite is not foolproof like quartz, so buyer beware. Just do your research.

GRANITE: Granite has lost its popularity lately, with its spotted appearance falling out of favor with designers and homeowners. However, I still like using the more solid-looking options such as honed Absolute Black and Jet Mist (which looks a lot like soapstone) in combination with marble, quartz, or quartzite. In a farmhouse-style home, this material can look just right.

FROM GOOD ENOUGH TO GREAT

A lot of times we've worked with clients who have a new, builder-designed kitchen or recently renovated space, but it's either very generic or just not "them." Perhaps some of the materials are nice but not something they LOVE. A great way to make the space feel more special is to make smaller changes—a new backsplash (but not new counters), or maybe just new lighting, hardware, and window treatments. A lot of times just painting the cabinetry can make your kitchen look completely renovated. These fixes cost significantly less than a renovation but still give you a fresh, updated look.

ABOVE: The kitchen before.

OPPOSITE: We updated this perfectly fine kitchen by simply installing a new backsplash, removing the decorative accents on the cabinets, updating the hardware, and replacing the light fixtures. It made a huge difference.

RIGHT: This breakfast nook is opposite the previous kitchen and had been its own room. We removed the dividing wall and added all new décor to make it feel fresh and family friendly.

FROM FRIDGE TO FRAME: KIDS' ART

"My kid could have done that!"—a common refrain from non–art lovers when looking at abstract art. And perhaps, yes, your child is the second coming of Jackson Pollock, but if not, you still should display their art with a little more flair than a magnet on the fridge! I adore taking Henry's "abstract" paintings and framing them in the same sort of frames as the other works and pictures on my gallery wall and mixing them in. Or, take a bunch of different artworks from your kids and frame them all in matching frames and hang together to create a singular display. It looks fantastic and keeps the fridge and pinboard from getting massively cluttered.

OPPOSITE: This family dining area is open to the family room and kitchen, but we made it feel more cozy by installing a large fixture and hanging a gallery of cherished art and prints on one wall.

ABOVE: My photographer, and friend, Sarah Winchester renovated her kitchen and used a big blank wall as a perfect space to display her children's artwork in a modern way.

PAIRING OFF

When dealing with open-concept spaces, you should think of things more cohesively—especially with lighting. Here's how we like to pair kitchen pendants with hanging fixtures for over the dining table when designing an open family space.

The round, closed orb of this pendant needs to be balanced by something with more openness and light. This linear lantern-style fixture is the perfect complement.

The slightly industrial vibe of these nickel pendants meets its match in a softer fabric pendant shade with more feminine curves.

With this popular globe-style glass pendant, I like to use something with multiple shades to bring a little interest into the space and add some visual weight as well.

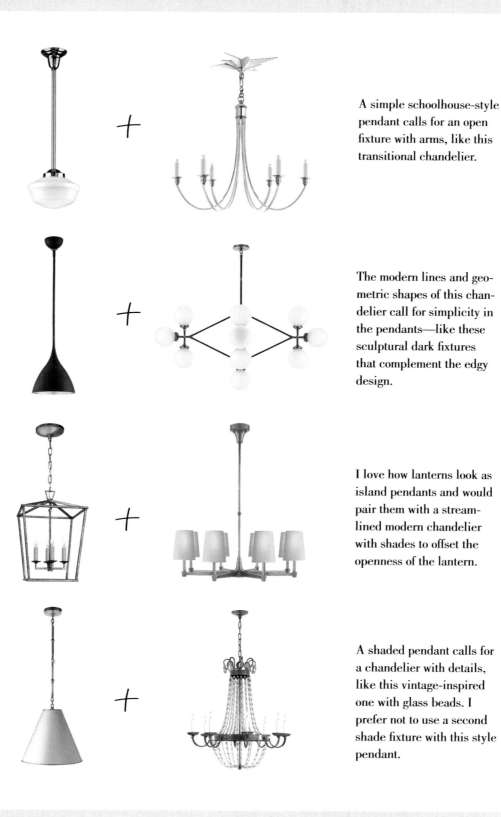

A simple schoolhouse-style pendant calls for an open fixture with arms, like this transitional chandelier.

The modern lines and geometric shapes of this chandelier call for simplicity in the pendants—like these sculptural dark fixtures that complement the edgy design.

I love how lanterns look as island pendants and would pair them with a streamlined modern chandelier with shades to offset the openness of the lantern.

A shaded pendant calls for a chandelier with details, like this vintage-inspired one with glass beads. I prefer not to use a second shade fixture with this style pendant.

OPPOSITE, TOP AND BOTTOM:
We optimized the space in this long and narrow kitchen by creating both a living and dining area, utilizing two islands as well as a cozy seating nook to provide plenty of seating options and space for their child to play.

LEFT: Historic details, like this marble mantel, contrast beautifully with the bright ephemera of busy family life!

SPLURGE VS. SAVE: THE KITCHEN

When it comes to the kitchen you have to balance function with beauty, so there are places you absolutely should be spending most of your money and places you can save and not have it impact the usefulness of the space.

SPLURGE: CABINETS—The cabinetry in your kitchen is the structural framework of your space, so buy the best you can afford. Quality hinges, inset doors (if you have the budget), and customized interiors for prime organization are all things you won't regret splurging on. If you aren't installing new cabinets, look into the best painter you can who sprays the doors offsite for a perfectly smooth finish.

SAVE: HARDWARE—This is such a great spot to save money, as I've seen some incredible hardware at big-box home stores for under four dollars apiece. Be sure to pick a style that works with the current holes drilled in the doors or you'll have to employ a professional to fill, sand, and refinish!

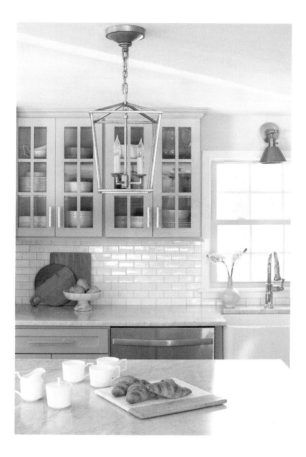

OPPOSITE: One of my former employees, Lindsey Hanson, transformed her dining area and kitchen by adding a gorgeous wood table and chandelier and using budget-friendly counter stools and chairs.

LEFT: In this space, the lights and counters were the splurge and the cabinets and tile were the saves!

SPLURGE: PENDANT LIGHTS—If you have an island or peninsula counter you plan to hang pendants over, consider them the jewelry of the kitchen. You want them to be beautiful as they will be one of the first things people notice! But be conscious of your illumination needs too, as some of the pretty fixtures that require vintage-style Edison bulbs don't actually give off a lot of light. If you need a lot of light, look for multi-bulb fixtures or those with white glass that conceal stronger bulbs.

SAVE: COUNTER STOOLS—Counter stools have a tendency to get trashed, so don't go spending a pretty chunk of your budget on them, unless they are solid wood or other nonupholstered material. There are so many wonderful, affordable options that you can easily find beautiful ones for very little money from many retail vendors.

ABOVE, LEFT TO RIGHT: Believe it or not, these were ready-made drapery panels bought on a discount site that Lindsey had our workroom pleat and hem! A stunning way to get a big look on a smaller budget. **|** The countertops we chose for this kitchen were quartzite, as the client wanted a marble look without the upkeep. A light green-gray tile backsplash was the perfect complement.

ABOVE: The window treatments add such warmth and polish to the open space. Layering woven wood shades under drapes is a timeless look we choose to use often.

SPLURGE: COUNTERS—As noted earlier, there are many options, and picking can be stressful. Be honest about what kind of lifestyle you have and choose what will stress you out the least, but invest smartly. Quartz is expensive but requires little upkeep, so it may be worth the extra cash.

ABOVE: This dreamy kitchen was the result of a meticulously thought-out renovation. The client fell in love with these pendants and so we paired them with a simple chandelier with shades.

SAVE: BACKSPLASH—Sometimes simple is best—you can't go wrong with a classic subway tile backsplash in a kitchen (I prefer those with contrasting grout). Not to mention, this style is beyond affordable and can be purchased just about anywhere from your local housewares shop to Home Depot.

ABOVE: Small pops of color can go a long way in a bright white kitchen. This client used quartzite for her counters and easy-to-clean bistro-style counter stools.

In this country kitchen we utilized a combination of brass and nickel tones, as well as an island that can seat the whole family. This client wanted to use marble but was nervous about staining, so we used it on the island and backsplash only but kept the main working surfaces honed granite. Island color is Benjamin Moore Chelsea Gray.

SPLURGE: FAUCET—Nothing is more frustrating than a poorly performing faucet in a kitchen. You want one that's solidly made (it should have some weight and heft to it, especially the sprayer) and has a reputation for being reliable. Also consider those with cool features that may come in handy, like the touchless faucets that let you simply tap the spout with your wrist or arm if your hands are dirty to get the water flowing.

SAVE: SINK—A beautifully crafted porcelain farm sink is lovely but may be too delicate for your needs or out of your budget. A drop-in stainless steel sink is easy to clean and resists scratching or chipping and is generally much more affordable.

OPPOSITE, TOP TO BOTTOM: Designer Patricia Knox combined a cottage sensibility with more modern touches, like these pendants, in this airy kitchen. ❙ Knox proves that even the smallest corner can function as a great banquette seating area!

ABOVE, LEFT TO RIGHT: A monochromatic kitchen by Jenn Feldman, with subway tile chosen to match the cabinetry color, shows us how bold can be very beautiful. The bright rug adds a great hint of contrasting color, too. ❙ When designing your kitchen, think about how you want it to function in even the smallest ways—like this genius cutting board built in above the trash can. Design by Jenn Feldman.

OPPOSITE: If you are nervous about committing to color in a big way in the kitchen, use lots of bright accents instead, like designer Dina Holland did in this kitchen through a rug, counter stools, and accessories.

ABOVE: Wallpapering the backs of glass cabinets is an easy (and removable) way to bring color into the kitchen. Designer Dina Holland went bold with this patterned choice.

SPLURGE: BUILT-IN SEATING—As I mentioned earlier, banquette seating adds amazing function and layout options to a kitchen and/or open-concept family living space. It costs a pretty penny not only to build the cabinetry associated with it but also to custom-upholster the cushioned seating. However, it's well worth it, especially when you can add in concealed storage underneath the seats.

ABOVE: Accents of navy in these bistro chairs and repeated in the custom roman shades balance out the color throughout the room.

SAVE: FREESTANDING BANQUETTE—If you really desire banquette-style seating, no need to spend on building it in if it's not in your budget. Many retailers offer freestanding pieces that not only cost a lot less but can be taken with you if you move. Great style without the commitment.

ABOVE, LEFT TO RIGHT: This sunny area off the kitchen was the perfect place for a casual dining setup—we used a ready-made banquette and comfy chairs to provide ample seating as the husband likes to work from this table often. ❙ This breakfast nook in Sarah Winchester's home serves as a transition from kitchen to formal dining and gives the kids (and Batman) a space to eat and play.

MUDROOMS, LAUNDRY & OTHER UTILITARIAN SPACES

The one phrase that can put chills down the spine of any parent is hearing a child mutter "Uh-oh!" from another room. My other personal favorite is "Mommy, come see!" That phrase has announced a puddle of pee on my nice carpet, marker on my walls, the dog covered in toys and shaking in a corner, and a whole juice box squeezed out on

OPPOSITE: Big or small, a mudroom is an essential feature for people with lots of stuff and busy lives. This beauty by Sarah Scales is done in the same wood tone as the kitchen cabinetry.

LEFT: The walls of this mudroom are Benjamin Moore Marlboro Blue and coordinate perfectly with the Katie Ridder wallpaper we chose for the adjoining bath.

the couch. I have never used my washer and dryer and vacuum more than I do now that Henry is in the picture, so the mudroom and laundry room are two spaces that are of utmost importance not only to me but to most of my clients as well. That doesn't mean they have to be big and fancy. Mine are both minuscule and well laid out and totally functional. And after NOT having either of those rooms before our second renovation, having them now still thrills me to bits. I used little touches to make them feel special, like fun wallpaper, art, and hardware. These are the kinds of spaces you really want to map out according to your lifestyle and not some dreamy idea of what your life could/should be.

KEY ELEMENTS OF
A GREAT MUDROOM

- DURABLE FLOORING: Since the mudroom can get messy (that is the point after all, right?), I like to use super-durable flooring when designing one. For mine, I chose a faux slate tile that is not only cheap but also really good-looking and easy to clean, thanks to the coordinating dark grout. Consider tile, stone, vinyl, plank, or wood with a large outdoor rug over it to protect from wet boots and the like.

- HOOKS & BINS: Wall hooks are some of the most-used accents in a mudroom—I installed a few large double hooks where we are most apt to toss a coat when we come in (I even installed one at Henry's height so he can get used to hanging up his own coat). Baskets and bins are the best way to corral small accessories like mittens and gloves, hats, scarves, and umbrellas. You can hide bins in the closet or find attractive ones and put them on the floor or in a cubby or shelf. It's ideal to give each member of the family his or her own bin to keep everyone's stuff separate.

- CUBBIES & CLOSETS: For multiple kids (or adults), it's hard to beat the functionality of a wall of built-in cubbies. Add attractive hooks for coats and baskets for smaller items.

- KEY & MAIL DROP: When you come in the house you need a place to drop the mail and store your keys (among other things!). Make sure there is a console, shelf, or chest somewhere in the vicinity if possible so these items don't end up all over your kitchen or living room. Trays and small boxes and baskets will help you keep small items organized.

- CHARGING STATION: When designing a new mudroom, we always try to work in some kind of charging station for devices (ideally USB ports in the shelves themselves) so gadgets can be kept in a central area.

ABOVE: To complement the stunning blue paint color, we chose graphic-patterned pillows and cushions for the small bench.

ORGANIZING THE FAMILY

If you have a busy family, you have to keep track of lots of little things—field trip permission slips, dry-cleaning receipts, the schedule for sports practices, bills, mail, dog leashes . . . SO. MUCH. STUFF. Whether it's in your mudroom, kitchen, pantry, or somewhere else, a little home-organizing station is always helpful. I think the most important items tend to be a family calendar (paper or on a whiteboard), message board/chalkboard, bulletin board, and something in which to sort mail (wall-mounted files work best for this). Attractive options abound and can be found anywhere, from your local discount home store to spots like Pottery Barn and Ballard Designs. You don't have to buy these items from an office supply store or hide them away because they're ugly. Making this area look attractive will encourage your family to use it.

OPPOSITE: A jaw-dropping patterned wood floor and painted dark cubbies and cabinets make for a dramatic mudroom full of style. Design by Patricia Knox.

TOUGHEST "LIVING WITH KIDS" DECORATING LESSON?

Things are just "things," no matter how sentimental we may feel about them. People are what matters. When my first son was a toddler, my husband was standing up holding him and my son reached over his shoulder and grabbed a beloved piece off the wall—my deceased grandmother's bowl that I'd always treasured—and promptly smashed it on the floor before either of us could stop him. I'd love to say that I was cool with it . . . but I wasn't. I was seething inside and possibly even more mad at myself for being upset at a baby! I got over it and realized that I was embarrassed about how much I cared about a thing, and nothing broken since has had much of an effect on me.

—LAUREN LIESS
LAUREN LIESS & CO.

ABOVE: The mudroom leads right into the playroom in this city brownstone. Lots of open shelving and baskets keep everything organized and even leave room for a spot to play hide-and-seek.

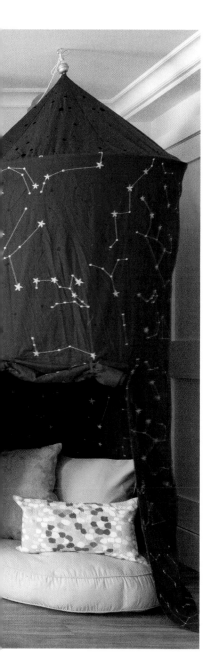

ABOVE: A mix of cabinetry and open cubbies make this mudroom a complete dream for the family. The faux stone floors aren't delicate and can withstand abuse.

OPPOSITE: My little laundry room is made to feel much grander by the use of this toile wallpaper and bird's-egg-blue ceiling.

LEFT: I think this laundry room/mudroom by Jenn Feldman is a perfect example of classic good design (and successful mixing of metals).

MAKING THE LAUNDRY ROOM PRETTY & FUNCTIONAL

My laundry room, like many rooms in my house, is small but efficient. It's a glorified closet that fits a washer and dryer and . . . that's about it! Luckily this space has a window for light and high ceilings, which help us maximize storage vertically via the shelves we installed above the machines. Because this room is open to the mudroom (we literally had not one spare inch for a pocket door) I wanted it to be pretty, so I chose a lively gray toile wallpaper for the walls and a bird's-egg-blue paint for the ceiling to bring some color and fun into a utilitarian space. Opposite the machines, I installed four wall hooks that I use to hang-dry items, as we don't have any space for a hanging rod. So far, it's worked out just fine for our little family.

TIPS:

- Use paint or pretty paper to dress up the walls of your laundry room (or utility closet!). It helps to have a nice, neat, and happy space to keep those dull tasks like laundry from being a total bummer.
- Store detergent pods and dryer sheets in cute jars and containers instead of leaving them in their packaging.
- Style up the ironing board with a cute patterned cover. Yes, they exist!
- If you don't have room for drying racks and rods, buy pretty hooks and put them wherever you can! Pair with some attractive velvet or wood hangers to dry shirts on!

ABOVE: Who says a laundry room can't be incredibly fun? This graphic sky-blue paper and even some original art create a cheery atmosphere.

This laundry room is a personal favorite—from the patterned cement-tile floors to the green cabinetry and honed Jet Mist granite counters.

ABOVE, LEFT TO RIGHT: Designer Nikki Dalrymple shows us what having fun with a space looks like by applying this sky-patterned wallpaper to an ethereal laundry room. ❙ This laundry room was functional but bare until we added some bold wallpaper to the mix and took it from basic to exceptional.

ABOVE: Ample folding space on the counter and a fun tile "rug" in this laundry room by Jenn Feldman mix dramatic and functional.

TWENTY PERFECT
NEUTRAL PAINT COLORS

SW HERON PLUME   SW EIDER WHITE   SW CITY LOFT   BM WIND'S BREATH

SW INCREDIBLE WHITE   F&B SLIPPER SATIN   BM CLASSIC GRAY   B SHOELACE

F&B SKIMMING STONE   BM BALBOA MIST   F&B CORNFORTH WHITE   BM GRAY OWL

A great neutral color that can carry from one room to the next (and down the halls) is a necessity in an open-floor-plan home, where cased openings don't always allow for each room to be its own color. Plus, keeping one nice neutral color in rooms that flow together really helps connect spaces and also makes the home feel calmer and brighter.

B SPUN WOOL   BM EDGECOMB GRAY   SW NATURAL TAN   B CAMPFIRE ASH

SW GOSSAMER VEIL   F&B SHADOW WHITE   BM ATHENA   BM REVERE PEWTER

KID
SPACES

a mommy makeover
(not the kind you think)

One of the most surprising things about motherhood for me has been the new sense of calm and peace it has given me. As a raging perfectionist who has struggled with anxiety for years, I, along with many others, predicted that motherhood, and all the unknowns and messiness that come along with it (both physical and emotional), would present a challenge for me. Some people probably thought I'd go absolutely bonkers. It made perfect sense to assume

OPPOSITE: I fell in love with this Susan Harter mural paper for Henry's nursery and built the design of the room around it.

that I might lose my mind. Children are sticky-fingered tornadoes of unpredictability. Life with kids is basically the antithesis of orderly, considered living, which was the kind of life I had become accustomed to for more than thirty-six years.

What actually happened was a surprise to many people who know me well, but most of all to me. Becoming a mother to my sweet little boy has brought me peace, renewed perspective, and greater focus. Certainly, it has not been all rainbows and unicorns and "Kumbaya" singalongs. Especially in the beginning, there were tears and regrets and hysterics surrounding how I was going to "do it all" and

do it perfectly. Henry's vulnerable little body scared me to death. His cries would rattle me to the bone, and breastfeeding caused a lot of stress and physical pain. There were nights I sat on the floor and cried, rocking him in my arms, feeling the crushing pressure of having a whole other person to care for and help mold into a loving, thoughtful human being. Or at least make sure he didn't become a serial killer. Sometimes it's best to keep expectations low, especially when running on little sleep.

In the early newborn stage, Henry had some challenges with gaining weight. Seeing my little baby looking gaunt or being poked and prodded by doctors drove home the fact

that little else matters other than the health and happiness of loved ones. Especially your own children. Those long days and nights of worrying about him incessantly and not being able to think about anything else changed me in a profound way. Until that point I hadn't been faced with anything that felt so dire, so truly scary. The experience made me realize that I needed to get my anxiety under control once and for all. All the things that stressed me out and made me so unhappy in my previous life seemed so insignificant and petty given this huge new reality check.

With a little work (weekly therapy and medication included), over time I began noticing subtle changes to my psyche and approach to just about everything in my life, not just caring for my child. As with most things, time heals. And once we were all getting sleep again and Henry was putting on the pounds, I somehow became a calmer person. The sort of person who doesn't get worked up about a chandelier

OPPOSITE, LEFT TO RIGHT: Me and newborn Henry. ❙ Giraffe hooks add to the animal theme in a subtle way and provide lots of spaces to hang bigger items.

ABOVE: Pale blues and grays (the walls are Benjamin Moore Alaskan Husky) mixed with natural linen tones make for a soothing yet graphically interesting room.

order being delayed eight weeks or the fact that the dog peed on the new carpet. AGAIN. As long as my son was healthy and happy, there was no pressing need to get absolutely hysterical. Having someone I care about more than anything else in the world gave me a frame of reference by which to measure all things.

That's not to say there aren't times that I feel worried, stressed, or overwhelmed, but my anxiety is at an all-time low, and I tend to feel much less of "the sky is falling" despair than I used to when things went a bit sideways. I may crack open the wine at 5:01 p.m. on a Tuesday, especially if I've had a crazy work day and then have to come home to a tantrum-throwing toddler, but when I get in bed at night I feel so much more relaxed. I don't worry about missing parties or dinners or feel like I need to be doing MORE to compete in this 24/7 social media world. I'm pretty content sitting in my house on a Saturday night watching *Curious George* AGAIN and getting in bed at 8:45 with a book. #happyloser.

This new approach to life has spilled over into the way I treat my home too. Yes, I still love pretty things, fabulously gorgeous fabrics and rugs, and lots of white and light colors. But they have a tough time coexisting with a naked toddler running around waving a melting chocolate ice cream cone (this has happened more than once in my house, believe it

or not). It's all fun and games until a custom Schumacher pillow gets stained.

I've found you can't get too bent out of shape about it all because it changes SO FAST. You start with one adorable vintage-inspired bassinet in the corner of your living room, and then seconds later the room is covered

OPPOSITE: A little modern abstract painting by Christina Baker above the linen glider adds grown-up flair to the nursery.

ABOVE: A large photograph by Sharon Montrose of a brave lion was one of my first purchases for the nursery. We love animals and wanted Henry to grow to love them as well.

in a sea of blinking, singing plastic nonsense. From the retina-searing Jumperoo (aka "Baby Vegas"), to the motorized swing we maybe used six times, to the hand-me-down walker that dented every baseboard in sight—we had it ALL. My custom-cut area rug was covered with a giant play mat that lit up and erupted in sound like a slot machine hitting the jackpot every time Henry touched it. My beautiful designer fabric pillows were splattered with breast milk. And my once-pristine kitchen was now home to a crazy huge drying rack, bottle warmer, piles of bibs, and a sterilizer. But I really could not have been happier about it. This was what I had always wanted. And wouldn't you know it, just as fast as it all came, it went as well. The breast milk rings are gone, and new marks have appeared.

Once all the big, plastic stuff was retired to the basement, I naïvely started thinking, "I don't need to change much in here—he'll just learn not to fall on the coffee table and we'll just deal." Until he started walking and took his first digger inches away from our sharp-edged brass and glass coffee table (which was, I now recognize, basically akin to a baby guillotine). In a flash, I pictured blood and punctured eyeballs. I swapped it out for an ottoman almost instantly. I had worked with many families before and always kept the children in mind when it came to safety and durability, but

until you are actually *living* with a teetering toddler who appears determined to maim himself, you just Do. Not. Get. It. While I believe you should teach children to respect nice and delicate things (I grew up in a house where we had a "fancy living room" we just knew was off-limits for playing), you can't rationalize with a fearless fifteen-month-old about the

danger and fragility of a glass table. But you don't need to turn your whole house into a primary-colored day-care zone either. There is a balance that exists between style and sanity.

In the past two and a half years, I have learned some hard lessons regarding the durability of certain fabrics (even some dubbed "stain resistant" really are no match for a smushed ground-in blueberry) and wallpaper (I bow down to vinyl grass cloth and washable crayons). When a client's little girl became sick and vomited on her fancy new broadloom rug, I discovered the limitations of even a small percentage of viscose. Currently, I'm learning that little boys will pee on EVERYTHING if they go around without a diaper for more than one-eighth of a second. But I also have learned that it is, in fact, just stuff. Sometimes pretty stuff. Often expensive stuff. But at the end of the day, that scribble of marker on your wall will not ruin your life. You CAN in fact flip that chair cushion over. And you certainly will not perish from that water ring left on your marble counter. I promise. Deep breaths! It will be okay.

Life is messy and kids are even messier, but we can all stand to be a little more grateful when it's a vase that breaks instead of a bone. And that these beautiful, perfectly imperfect homes we're creating will become the stage on which their memories will forever be set.

OPPOSITE: I got a lot of grief online about using this Lucite bookshelf in the nursery, but it's anchored to the wall and Henry has yet to try to climb it two and half years later!

ABOVE: I made sure not to forget about his little closet! I used a wood-grain wallpaper from France on the walls and a great striped schoolhouse fixture on the ceiling to add some pattern.

NURSERIES & BEDROOMS

I t is completely possible (and fiscally smart) to create a nursery that looks adorable and appropriate for an infant but has the ability to transition into an older child's room with minimal investment. Choosing a wallpaper, for instance, that will as easily work with baby toys and stuffed animals as it will with race cars or a favorite Disney character is a smart choice as that is not an easy, or affordable, item to update. I always tell clients that the nursery is also for the PARENTS to enjoy, so make selections that are safe and entertaining for baby but also soothing and attractive for you too. Don't worry that the decoration of their room won't properly stimulate brain activity and therefore keep them from getting into Harvard someday. It can be whatever you want it to be. And I found that it helps, even just a little bit, to have some nice art to stare at when you're soothing a crying baby at three a.m.

OPPOSITE: This nursery was designed around the parents' honeymoon safari, employing bold colors and natural textures to create a space that guarantees smiles!

FORM & FUNCTION:
CREATING A NURSERY THAT LASTS BEYOND INFANCY

CRIBS: Picking a gender-neutral crib allows you to use it for more than one child. Also selecting one that turns into a toddler bed is a great way to get the most bang for your buck. Simple lines made of white wood are super-safe bets.

OPPOSITE, LEFT TO RIGHT: The animal-patterned fabric for the roman shades was one of the first selections for this space. The glider is covered in a durable blue woven that coordinates with the navy leopard rug. **|** In the closet of this nursery we selected a leaf-patterned paper to create a special nook inspired by the jungle.

ABOVE: We covered the walls in vinyl grass cloth and hung the homeowners' own photographs flanking the stunning brass canopy crib. We also sourced vintage safari helmets to add a little whimsy.

ABOVE: This baby girl's nursery was done with a vintage sensibility in mind—from the pink scenic paper to the vintage rug and brass crib.

ABOVE: This large antique French armoire creates tons of extra storage (and fit into the space by the skin of its teeth!). The rug was found on Etsy. Wall color is Benjamin Moore Melted Ice Cream.

COLOR SCHEMES: Whether pregnant and not finding out the gender (pure insanity in my control-freak book) or perhaps wanting a room to be able to switch between siblings of opposite genders later on, picking a more neutral color scheme for a room is a safe bet. For a base color try sticking to grays/neutrals or navy (great for either a girl or boy) and then adding accents in bolder colors in smaller ways like pillows, art, and bedding. My current favorite "go-either-way" scheme is grays, linen, and a mossy green or chartreuse.

RUGS: As mentioned earlier, there are certain materials that work best in spaces that are childcentric. For durability, wool and indoor/outdoor materials are best. Shag-style rugs, while super soft for baby to roll on, will be a nightmare to clean any sort of "accident" off of and also shed as much as a pet dog. So instead I like to layer a soft sheepskin rug on top of something flatter and easier to clean. If you stick to stripes, geometrics, or neutrals as your base, you can use that rug for a very long time through many stages of your child's life. I also like to make sure the rug covers most of the floor to ensure the largest play space possible.

PAINT & PAPER: Paint is the easiest thing to change in a room, so go ahead and pick something sweet and soft for the baby years; you can make it a bolder shade once they get a bit older. Paper is a bit harder to change, so try doing just one accent wall in case the pattern becomes something you (or your child) tire of over time. Henry's accent paper is so neutral and not age specific that it will work even if that room turns into a guest room someday. Also consider some of the newer removable wallpapers for a very low commitment choice. And don't forget about the ceiling. It's a great spot for paper or a cool paint application, like stripes or stars.

OPPOSITE: By covering all the walls of this nursery in a happy patterned paper, designer Colleen Simonds created a unique and cheerful space.

ABOVE: Our clients loved the look of de Gournay paper but knew this wasn't their forever home, so we framed two panels above the crib in their nursery so they can take it with them wherever they move next!

ABOVE: Preppy and bohemian accents mix well against the backdrop of a wall painted in Sherwin-Williams Intimate White.

ABOVE: Combining various stripes and plaids with leather and wood makes this little boy's room masculine but still youthful. Design by Jenn Feldman.

OPPOSITE: Jenn Feldman's use of a silhouetted animal print mixed with extra-wide stripes is a great use of pattern.

ABOVE: A bold but traditionally patterned paper looks modern when paired with a custom-upholstered glider and ottoman and color-blocked roman shade by Dana Ferraro of Molly Patton Design.

WINDOW TREATMENTS: These are expensive if made custom to your windows, so spend once smartly. Solid shades or draperies (I like white with a colored trim or border—which also can easily be switched out) need to last way beyond the nursery years. When selecting these, imagine if they would work in a teenager's room or even a guest room, if one day this space will be used for that. Redoing window treatments is painful, so hiring a professional is highly advised! If you don't know where to begin finding a local workroom, check out online resources that will even send you samples to try out before ordering.

ABOVE: In this tiny city nursery, designer Emily Butler maximized the amount of functional furniture, making it usable as a guest space in a pinch.

LEFT: Designer Kate Coughlin gorgeously paired powder-blue walls with glossy red trim and a fun star-pattern fabric to craft a chic playroom scheme.

Building a daybed and closet space under an awkward ceiling slope is a genius use of space by Lindsey Hanson.

ABOVE, LEFT TO RIGHT: In Lindsey Hanson's nursery a gorgeous floral wallpaper that mixes light blue and pink is complemented by an abstract work by Christina Baker. ❙ Who hasn't dreamt of a cozy bed nook with drapes and a reading light? The wall color is Benjamin Moore Melted Ice Cream.

ABOVE: An IKEA closet system is perfect for storing tiny clothes, and the sliding barn doors mean no need to leave room for the door swing (important in a tiny room).

STORAGE: I love a good bookcase in a nursery. It's great to surround kids with books from the time they are born, of course, but I also use them to display framed pictures and hold extra supplies (just buy some cute canvas bins or baskets and load 'em up! Later on they'll corral toys and Legos). Just an important reminder to ALWAYS secure furniture like this to the wall to avoid dangerous falls. Your local home improvement store has wall-fastening kits if the pieces don't come with them.

OPPOSITE: Colleen Simonds created a jaw-dropping kids' room by covering the walls in this Quadrille paper in a funky green color.

ABOVE: The deep-green walls of this bunk room (Benjamin Moore's Webster Green) are a dramatic backdrop to warm wood furniture and a modern photograph by Sharon Montrose.

ADDITIONAL FURNITURE: The one purchase I regret is my too-upright glider. Take my advice and buy a glider that also reclines. You're going to spend a lot of time in that room, often half asleep. I now tell ALL my clients to go this route. For a changer, I prefer to buy an actual dresser that can be used in any kind of bedroom and place a changing pad on top for the diaper stage. If the room is large enough, I always like to add a daybed, as it's a fabulous place to read books together and then also can serve as their big-kid bed or a guest bed.

ABOVE, LEFT TO RIGHT: This vintage rug was another Etsy score and looks amazing with the modern changing table and buffalo-check blackout shades with pom-pom trim. ▮ A slipcovered glider and wall ledges for books create a cozy reading nook. Wall color is Benjamin Moore Dreamy Cloud.

OPPOSITE: A pretty queen bed in front of a custom-colored mural paper creates both a "big girl" space as well as a nursery in this room.

ABOVE: This was at one time an entertainment center built-in, but we retrofitted it to be a reading nook by adding a custom cushion, pillows, and a statement mirror.

LEFT: Modern art, bright books, and that VERY popular stuffed giraffe add an air of youthfulness.

OPPOSITE: This client really wanted an unexpected space for her little girl, which we did by cladding the walls in this overscale print grass cloth and pairing it with a bamboo daybed.

BEST PIECE OF ADVICE YOU GIVE TO CLIENTS WHO HAVE KIDS?

I like to have a cozy corner with a good light to read by. Children love to be read to, so I try to add a small sofa or chair and ottoman to snuggle up in.

—KATIE RIDDER
KATIE RIDDER INC.

ART: When I was decorating Henry's nursery, I invested in one large piece of art—a photograph of a lion—that I loved in his nursery but also could easily picture in his "big-boy room." There is a ton of great affordable art out there these days for kids, but don't hesitate to put something more "grown-up" in a baby room. The dichotomy of "adult" and "baby" is a good tension to create. We LOVE using abstract pieces in nurseries. Plus the bright colors and shapes are great for baby's developing eyes.

ABOVE, LEFT TO RIGHT: A combination of navy, light blue, and gray is both masculine and soothing. The walls are painted Benjamin Moore Slate Blue. ▌ A modern metal dresser is topped with sculptural rope lamps and a large-scale lion photograph by Sharon Montrose.

AN ANTIQUES WARNING

I love using vintage or antique items in a kids' room to give it a little more interest. However, you need to be careful about what exactly those antiques are made of, as standards have changed. For example, we had a set of Henry's great-grandfather's blocks in his room and an alert blog reader cautioned me to check them for lead paint. I bought a simple lead paint test kit online and lo and behold—the blocks tested positive for lead. Any painted furniture should be tested and also examined for sturdiness and safety before being placed in a child's space.

ABOVE, LEFT TO RIGHT: A mod ceiling fixture and floor-to-ceiling wall of book ledges add a contemporary twist to this little guy's space by Sarah Winchester. ❚ Nods to pretty and nautical style in this room by Emily Butler transcend all age groups.

LIGHTING: Having options for lighting in a nursery or a kid's bedroom is really important—an overall ceiling fixture or recessed lighting is a good base (a dimmer is a big plus), but you'll also want low lighting options for nursing or snuggle time and a light by the chair or glider for reading. Utilizing a mix of floor lamps, sconces, and table lamps will accomplish this—just make sure you use LED bulbs so the fixtures don't get hot to the touch.

OPPOSITE: This room has very high ceilings but lots of tricky slants and windows, so the pair of twin beds had to be placed in front of the windows, which created a nice symmetry. The light fixture was custom-made.

ABOVE, LEFT TO RIGHT: The safari wallpaper on just the bed wall has major impact and gave us a palette of orange, navy, and sky blue to work with. ❙ A hip, modern rug is soft and lovely underfoot. Image from Jenn Feldman.

BLACK IT OUT: A GUIDE TO SAFE & STYLISH WINDOW TREATMENTS

Window treatments tend to be a major investment in any room, but given that naptime is made easier with great window coverings, you may be more apt to spring for them in the nursery than even your own room. I recall at one point duct-taping the edges of my roman shades to the window frame to make it extra dark because I didn't think through the placement of the shades properly. I ended up layering drapes over roman shades to block light most effectively. You can also look into roller or cellular shades with side channels if light seepage is an issue—but best to layer a roman shade or drapes over these as they aren't the most attractive. The main concern for children when it comes to window treatments is the cords—make sure you either buy cordless shades (most places offer them) or use a continuous loop pull that attaches to the window frame. Children have died from being strangled by these string pulls, so remove them to avoid any cause for worry!

OPPOSITE, TOP LEFT TO RIGHT: You don't always have to go bold with color in a nursery for it to be fun—subtle tones of neutrals and light blues feel rich and calming. Design by Lovejoy Interiors. ❙ I adore how this small-pattern fabric worked as a roman shade when paired with an inset tape trim. Ageless and timeless, which makes the investment in custom treatments worthwhile.

OPPOSITE, BOTTOM: I love the combination of light blue and red, and in this boy's room we added lots of leather accents to the mix to make it a little bit more grown-up.

BABY TO BIG KID

Creating a room that has childlike spirit
& staying power

ART: Look for modern takes on your kid's favorite things, from hobbies to TV characters (Etsy has some creative prints of popular TV characters done in an attractive way). Use frames that allow you to replace contents with ease—as we all know, "favorites" change pretty quickly as kids grow.

WALLPAPER: You can use wallpaper in a kid's room without fear if it's a fun print that will never feel too babyish. Consider removable or vinyl versions too, as they tend to be more durable (or at least easy to take down!). Or do just one accent wall or the ceiling to keep it more affordable.

FURNITURE: Getting rid of a changing table leaves a big gap in the room, so pick storage pieces that are timeless and ageless. You can even consider vintage items like wood dressers, but swap the hardware for something a little more youthful.

BED: Most of my clients skip the toddler bed entirely and go right to a regular bed (full size or queen typically) to avoid having to buy another bed in a few years. Another great option is doing a twin daybed with a trundle—pull it out when they are toddlers to cushion any falls, and when they get older it's perfect for sleepovers.

FABRICS: Like wallpaper, the goal is to select patterns and colors that have a sense of whimsy and fun but aren't too juvenile or something that will get tired over time. Ageless prints and patterns like stripes, florals, paisley, and graphics can easily see you from toddler to teen if chosen smartly. And try to involve your kids in the decision-making process so they feel ownership of the room.

STORAGE: Needs change as kids grow, so your need to house toys may turn to more books, art supplies, and the like. Investing in a bookshelf is a great idea—you can use bins early on and then remove them to make room for more books and display space. And when you no longer need a glider, a small desk is great for art projects (and then, someday, homework!).

OPPOSITE: Who says a race-car bed can't be stylish? Letting kids chime in with their desires is an important part of creating a space everyone loves.

LEFT: Black and white is a stunning combination as an accent to this statement wallpaper in a room by Jessie Miller.

GIVING THEM A SAY

It may seem silly, but no matter the age of the child, I like to communicate with him about what HIS desires are for his room. Maybe it's just a color, or a pattern, a piece of art or a favorite toy, but I feel children should have a say in the creation of their own spaces. While we avoid decorating a room based on a favorite TV show character or cartoon (after all, those trends can change on a whim), you can incorporate current favorites into a room in a way that is easy to change. We've found modern-art interpretations of beloved Disney characters on Etsy and installed them on the wall in frames that allow for the prints to be swapped out. We've also found photographers who will take portraits of favorite toys and print them large-scale on acrylic, which is a really cool memento to have once the child gets older.

LEFT: A nook with a floor-to-ceiling window is made into a quaint study area with a large blackout roman shade for blocking out light at night.

OPPOSITE: A subtle star wallpaper and violet accents make for a sweet toddler girl's room.

MY CHILDHOOD BEDROOMS

My first memory of my room as a child was a bright, eyeball-searing green cut-pile carpet. It was in our house when my parents bought it before I was born and I remember thinking it looked like a freshly cut lawn. I had a shiny brass bed that squeaked when I rolled over, and there was a tiny door to the attic where I was convinced monsters lived, but where I also had ample Barbie storage space, so I had to get over that. As I got older, the décor changed. In middle school, my room blossomed into a Laura Ashley festival of 80s color—a matching purple-and-yellow floral print on everything from balloon shades (remember those beauties?) to wallpaper and bedding. I thought it was the epitome of elegance. I had a cute little window seat and a dressing room with a vanity where I would organize my Wet n Wild makeup in my pink-and-purple Caboodles while my crimper was warming up (let the evidence show that I'm

so old). Later on, my room reflected my one true passion in life: *Beverly Hills, 90210*. I made a collage of magazine cutouts on the wall above my bed and, I'm embarrassed to say, had pillowcases with Brandon and Dylan's faces on them (of course, Dylan was my preferred place to rest my head, as the bad boy always wins). I remember a lot of poignant moments in my life happening in these rooms. And while they weren't perfect or even pretty at times, these rooms served as comforting spaces I could express myself in and call my own.

THE MULTIFUNCTION ROOM

As kids get bigger, their needs change dramatically, and soon a room has to function not only as a place to sleep and play but also do schoolwork and enjoy hobbies. Creating little "nooks" within the room to read and study allows them the space to spread out but also organize and focus themselves better. If you are lucky enough to have a bonus room, a great use for that kind of extra space is to create a combined kids' study/guest room so they can do homework in a room without tempting toys and games, and the space will still be elegant enough to function as a guest room when you have friends or family come to visit.

OPPOSITE, LEFT TO RIGHT: An extra-wide desk creates space for two kids to work at this tabletop. Wide-border drapes define the windows ❚ A tall, skinny rolling bookshelf fits perfectly between drapery panels and provides additional book storage.

ABOVE: This room serves as a guest space as well as a study for this client's daughter—we created a space appropriate for both uses.

SPLURGE VS. SAVE: KIDS' ROOMS

SPLURGE: BIG-KID BED—When a child is ready to move to a "big-kid bed," a lot of our clients prefer to invest in a nice full- or queen-size bed in a style that will easily transition with the child as he gets older (and bigger!). And once the child is off to college, this bed can serve as a guest bed as well. So buy this piece in a nonjuvenile style.

ABOVE: In this young boy's room we used a sailboat paper by Katie Ridder and coordinated it with a navy headboard and bordered roman shades,

SAVE: CRIB—There are so many amazingly designed cribs at such great prices these days; spending on a crazy-expensive one isn't the best use of money when on a budget. Stick to something white with clean lines and use other items in the room to add detail and dimension. Also, buying a gender-neutral style ensures you can use it for your second (or sixth) child!

ABOVE: By applying grass cloth to the walls and painting the trim navy, designer Kate Coughlin created an appealing space for any age.

SPLURGE: WINDOW TREATMENTS—I may be repeating myself here, but it's for good reason: spend on high-quality blackout window treatments for your kids' rooms. You will not regret it. Layering treatments may be your best bet, so look at roller or roman shades paired with drapes for a luxe look and max effectiveness.

ABOVE: This apple green and fuchsia room by Anna Burke is perfect for anyone—from a preteen to adult. Note the painted checkerboard floor—a great option instead of a rug!

OPPOSITE, TOP TO BOTTOM: A beachy boy's room done in wood-plank wallpaper and lots of crisp white and navy by designer Cecilia Walker looks nautical but still very modern. ▌ A pair of navy upholstered headboards are punched up with red accents in our client's son's bedroom.

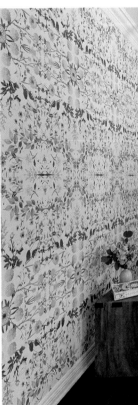

SAVE: WALLCOVERINGS—Themed or age-specific wallpaper is a BIG commitment, and in my experience kids don't fare well with "commitment." A stripe or basic pattern is okay, but paying to have novelty wallpaper removed and then reinstalled or painting over it is very costly.

SPLURGE: RUG—A high-quality rug, sized generously to your child's room, is a worthy investment. They'll be playing on it, rolling on it—maybe even peeing on it. So something high quality in a material that is easy to clean is crucial. We recommend 100 percent wool rugs, which offer coziness and are easy to clean.

OPPOSITE: Pale pink gingham walls and brass accents look sweet but still mature enough for a tween/teen girl. Design by Nicole Reynolds.

ABOVE, LEFT TO RIGHT: Teen rooms don't have to be loud and brash. This room by Amy Sklar shows how modern design and funky patterns can look sophisticated yet fun. ❚ This mod hanging chair looks perfectly cool against the graphic floral wallpaper in this teen girl's room.

SAVE: ACCESSORIES—Spend less on things that are easy to swap out, such as bedding, pillows, and lamps. Not only do children change their minds about what they like, they may break or damage these items, and replacing them shouldn't be taxing on your wallet.

ABOVE, LEFT TO RIGHT: By placing beds and larger furniture against the walls, like in this room by Julie Richard, you leave ample floor space for activities and play. ▌ Nothing is more charming than a pair of unique and bright twin beds. This pairing of crisp red, pink, and hints of blue is a great palette that isn't overused. Design by Robin Henry Studio.

OPPOSITE: For her thirteenth birthday, we decorated this teen girl's bedroom in fun shades of chartreuse and aqua blue, a scheme that will look great through adulthood.

BATHROOMS

When creating a bathroom that is specifically to be used by kids, we focus on a few key elements: a crisp, cheery palette (but nothing too cute or precious), materials that are easy to clean, and lots of places to store things (bath toys seem to procreate like rabbits in my house!). I also always suggest adding a hand shower in kids' baths and showers to make cleaning the tub or walls (and rinsing shampoo or dirt off the kids themselves) much easier!

OPPOSITE: We chose this bright graphic paper as a colorful complement to an all-white bathroom. Nautical-inspired lights and mirror add some unique texture and style!

THINK ABOUT THE FUTURE

While your kids may be small now, they won't be forever. So while you want to make this space cute and kid-sized for them now, always consider the future. This bathroom will either be used by teenagers or as a guest bathroom for adults down the road. Keep all hard goods (tile, vanities, lighting, and plumbing fixtures) classic and timeless. We like to add kid-specific color through paint and wallpaper as well as shower curtains and towels.

OPPOSITE: A bathroom clad floor to ceiling in Brunschwig & Fils Les Touches paper is a spirited choice for this family space by Grapevine Interiors.

ABOVE, LEFT TO RIGHT: A small-scale wave-patterned paper is fun but not juvenile, and the plate-glass mirror nearly disappears on top of it! Design by Cecilia Walker. ❚ We added color to this boy's bathroom by making a shade from a favorite Peter Dunham star-print fabric.

OPPOSITE: In this playroom bath we had a custom-made vanity painted a gorgeous blue to coordinate with the cement-tile floor. Leather pulls add a casual and fun texture to the otherwise simple design.

LEFT: The devil is in the details—like this perfectly coordinated trim on the roman shade with the blue wallpaper pattern.

ACCENTS ARE IMPORTANT

Art and mirrors make a HUGE difference in a bathroom, so these are the things you may want to go more age specific on, as they are easy to swap out. If you don't need a medicine cabinet, use a fun and spunky wall mirror to add some personality. For littles who need a boost to get to the sink, scour sites like Etsy for custom-made step stools to coordinate with your décor.

WHAT TO AVOID

One of my biggest regrets in Henry's bathroom was using bright white grout on the floor. It got dingy and dirty within months. I now like to specify a light-gray-beige grout with marble floors as it hides more dirt (and missed shots at the toilet). The fewer the grout lines, the easier they are to clean as well, so opt for larger-scale floor tiles in bathrooms that receive heavy kid traffic. And stick to quartz vanity tops. I like to pair bright solid white with colored vanities as there is literally NO staining and it looks super clean.

OPPOSITE, LEFT TO RIGHT: In this little girl's bathroom we applied a graphic paper in the palest gray and white and installed a lacquered bamboo mirror to create a space that was simple but pretty. ❙ We dressed up the existing finishes in this bathroom with new paint, lighting, a medicine cabinet, and a bright yellow striped shower curtain.

ABOVE, LEFT TO RIGHT: We selected this whimsical patterned fabric to coordinate with the gray-blue vanity in this bathroom. ❙ Classic accessory choices create a timeless space, but we added some cute art to make it feel more youthful.

OPPOSITE: A large-scale modern basketweave tile coordinates beautifully with this gray vanity and chain-link mirror. A tiny vintage rug is used in place of a standard bathmat!

LEFT: We used a pale blue paper to perk up this basement bathroom off the playroom and mudroom that the kids frequent but made sure it was elegant enough for guests to use as well.

CREATING STORAGE

Pedestal sinks are great in small bathrooms because they are streamlined and can make a space feel larger—but they also create issues when you need places to store stuff. We typically use vanities, even tiny ones, in all guest or kids' bathrooms for this reason. But if you prefer a pedestal sink, or if you've inherited a pedestal sink that you can't replace, be creative—install floating shelves above the toilet to hold baskets that can conceal smaller items and bath toys. You can install a wall-mounted medicine cabinet. We've even added skirts to pedestal sinks so that our clients can hide items underneath in a pinch.

PLAYROOMS

You are lucky if you have a dedicated play space for your kids—meaning a room in which to keep all their toys so they are away from the rest of the house. We were fortunate to be able to renovate our basement into a playroom for Henry. It allows us to keep bigger toys (like train sets and a slide) in a separate room and it also is a space that allows for free play and creativity. In a pinch, this space serves as another guest room, which is huge when you live in a smaller home. We made the mistake of installing a beverage fridge in the space, which seemed like a great idea pre-Henry. But as he got older he'd constantly open it up and try to grab a beer, so we removed it and now the empty space is the perfect spot for storing his big cardboard blocks!

OPPOSITE: A custom built-in creates a place to store (and hide) toys in this basement playroom we designed. Accents in bright yellow add a sunny pop of color to the gray and white scheme.

BEAUTIFYING THE BASEMENT

Just as we did in our home, many of our clients use their basement as a family space that combines a playroom with more adult-friendly features, like a bar, a kitchenette, or even a basketball court! If your basement has decent ceiling height, think about how you can renovate the space to be family friendly. It will add valuable square footage, and you can get creative decorating because it's not open to other areas of your home!

OPPOSITE: We have added a small playscape to this space as Henry has gotten older, but the room still remains a spot we can all enjoy!

CLOCKWISE, FROM TOP LEFT: In my basement, a sofa with soft arms and an acrylic table are safe choices for rambunctious kids. Sconces allow for play without worry that a lamp will be knocked over! ▮ A sliding barn door lets us close off the space and also adds a nice warm texture in combination with the faux wood vinyl plank flooring. ▮ We used IKEA finds mixed with high-end accents like the fun forest-themed wallpaper.

TOUGHEST "LIVING WITH KIDS" DECORATING LESSON?

No glass-topped tables, ever. Poppy dropped something on a coffee table in our bedroom and it shattered into a million pieces. No one was hurt, but the table now has a new stone top.

—NATE BERKUS
INTERIOR DESIGNER AND AUTHOR

OPPOSITE: Behind the sectional is a basketball court (and a bonus soccer goal). We coordinated the gym flooring with the vinyl plank as well as the paint.

ABOVE: This basement is a large recreational area for the whole family, with a huge sectional and various ottomans for sitting and kicking up your feet.

In another area of this space is a full bar and a bar-height seating area for snack time and entertaining when friends and their parents come over!

ABOVE: A raised area acts as a stage for these lucky kids in this playroom designed by Nicole Hirsch. The orange ceiling defines the space and makes it pop.

OPPOSITE, TOP TO BOTTOM: Playrooms and family spaces are spots where you can feel more comfortable making bold choices, like this orange sofa and ottoman. ❙ Designer Nicole Hirsch had a huge space to work with and created different zones for the kids to play in—from a gym station to a living area.

TOUGHEST "LIVING WITH KIDS" DECORATING LESSON?

We kept our light linen sofa and it was completely destroyed after three years. I had this notion that I would somehow be immune to the throw up, pen marks, dirt, and chocolate fingerprints. I was wrong! It just happens. We replaced the linen with a leather sofa and it has been a very good decision! Now I understand why all of our clients with children always request a cognac leather sofa—they hide everything and age more gracefully.

—SHEA MCGEE
STUDIO MCGEE

STORAGE, STORAGE, STORAGE

A playroom can easily start looking like a tornado whipped through it if you don't create an easy organization system for the kids to use to put things away. If you can splurge for a built-in, it's a great investment. If not, there are plenty of retailers that make freestanding "built-ins" you can place on a large open wall to mimic the look for a fraction of the cost. Also consider systems sold at places like the Container Store or IKEA, which offer great stackable drawers and bins you can label in a pretty way for each set of Legos or Barbie accessories. Use matching organizational items to make it look especially tidy and clean.

WHAT CLICHÉ/OUTDATED ADVICE DO YOU WISH PEOPLE WOULD STOP LISTENING TO WHEN IT COMES TO DECORATING A FAMILY HOME?

We hate when we hear people say they won't decorate "until the kids are old enough"! The time will never be ideal and you (as parents) should live in a nicely decorated home NOW!

—SUYSEL DEPEDRO CUNNINGHAM & ANNE MAXWELL FOSTER
TILTON FENWICK

OPPOSITE, LEFT TO RIGHT: A basement kitchenette is a great way to keep snacks and beverages at hand when your play space is on another level from the kitchen. Design by Nicole Hirsch. ▮ A wall of cubbies is made into a large-scale art installation with a unique custom paint job! Design by Nicole Hirsch.

ABOVE: Instead of a play table in the middle of the room, designer Nicole Hirsch used brackets along a long wall to create a counter-style activity table complete with colorful stools.

SACRIFICE A SPACE

If you don't have a playroom, consider making an unused or rarely used room, like the formal dining room, into a temporary playroom. Your home should work for your lifestyle now, and if you use the dining room twice a year and struggle with not having a playroom, then put your furniture in storage and turn it into one. You can always turn it back later!

OPPOSITE: This room was a rarely used dining space, so designer Sarah Scales helped her client turn it into a temporary playroom while her kids were young.

ABOVE: The rug in this space works now while it's a playroom but is stylish enough to work when the client decides to make it a dining room again. Design by Sarah Scales.

LEFT: While the shelves currently hold toys and books, they will eventually hold china when the room turns back into a dining area someday!

OPPOSITE: If a Ping-Pong table will get more use by your family than a formal dining table or living room, then by all means—do it! Design by Jenn Feldman.

CLOCKWISE, FROM TOP LEFT: Perhaps you won't use an office space but have a room that is "supposed" to be one? Instead you could make it a fun play space for the family like designer Cecilia Walker did here. ▌ We selected a bright patterned fabric to make pinboards above each desk in this formal library turned play area. Ample shelving allows for great toy and book storage and display. ▌ A love of music and guitars is simply and beautifully displayed in this laid-back space by Darci Hether.

This room was a dark wood-paneled library off the family room but our clients wanted it to be a playroom. We painted the paneling gray and added in colorful accents so it would feel youthful but still coordinate with the adjoining room.

GO BIG OR GO HOME

I had so much fun designing our playroom because it allowed me to use some bolder colors and patterns than I would use in my own living room. Have fun with this space—paint a whole wall with chalkboard paint or use a really fun wallpaper. Or perhaps it's a color scheme you're too nervous to try in a more central room in the home. Also consider hanging large-scale art, installing a hanging chair, or working a teepee into the mix. Make this a space the kids will really want to be in, so they don't try to bring all their toys into YOUR space.

OPPOSITE, LEFT TO RIGHT: Bright colors and patterns on a base of solid neutrals makes for a happy playroom for kids and parents, like this one by Grapevine Interiors. ❙ A built-in sofa with storage drawers beneath the seats is a great way to maximize seating and storage. Design by TBHCo.

ABOVE, LEFT TO RIGHT: Books can act as wall décor when displayed on floor-to-ceiling shelving like in this space designed by TBHCo. ❙ Coordinate solid, durable window-seat cushions (for curious little ones) with patterned wallpaper like in this space by Grapevine Interiors.

OPPOSITE, TOP TO BOTTOM: A round ottoman and geometric wool rug are durable and stylish choices for a playroom the whole family can relax in. ▮ A comfy sectional is key in any playroom—for kids to watch movies on or parents to kick back on while watching their kids play. Patterned pillows add a joyful vibe.

ABOVE, LEFT TO RIGHT: You can create special nooks for fun hobbies in any room, like this little painting "studio" in a room by designer Julie Richard. ▮ Custom-made ottomans with storage are a sneaky and stylish way to conceal toys. These are by designer Anna Matthews.

a note from dad
ANDREW'S REFLECTIONS ON FATHERHOOD

Henry is just over two and a half years old. Fatherhood is every cliché ever written. That I'd jump in front of a bullet to save him goes without saying. I'd shoot my foot if I thought it would make him giggle for a moment. When it comes to Henry, every nerve ending is on high alert. Every emotion is amplified. Every action, decision, and moment is more meaningful. Every morning when he wakes up asking for "Daddy" is like Christmas. Every night when he finally goes to sleep is also like Christmas. I can't imagine loving anything more intensely. I can't imagine how it feels for Erin. She created him, after all.

Fatherhood is just getting started. There are so many experiences I want to share. His first game at Fenway. The first time he sees the Eiffel Tower. The first time he scores a goal. The first time he gets his heart broken. The first time he fails after giving it his all. There are so many places I want to show him. We're going to do a drive across country. I've never been on safari and he's the perfect excuse. There are so many movies he needs to appreciate, from *Star Wars* to *Caddyshack* to *The Godfather: Part 2*; I have a whole list. There are so many things I have to teach him and even more I have to let him learn for himself. But the truth is, I am the one who gets to have all the new experiences. I am the one learning every day.

Watching him grow, seemingly every minute, makes everything worthwhile.

While the gray may be coming quicker now, kids do keep you young. It's a second chance to relive and improve upon your own childhood. There is a constant internal struggle between wanting to map out the perfect path and letting him grow up. Erin and I were brought up differently in certain respects. Erin had more structure and I was pushed out of the nest. We both were brought up by loving parents who believed what they were doing was the best way to raise us. And they were right. If Erin and I agree on anything, it is that a balance of those two practices is how we want to raise Henry.

I can't sum up fatherhood in a couple of paragraphs. I can't sum it up period. Being "Daddy" is the best. Being a parent is f*cking hard. I suppose that finding a balance between the two is the goal of fatherhood. I'll do my best to enjoy every second of this journey.

OPPOSITE, TOP TO BOTTOM: Wallcoverings are my favorite way to add interest to a space and make it special, like this large-scale map wallcovering used by designer Kate Coughlin. ▌ A fun playroom doesn't HAVE to be colorful—graphic black and white done in a variety of patterns makes this playroom by Jessie Miller just as exciting!

KIDS' ROOM
PAINT COLORS

BM HALE ORANGE   F&B LULWORTH BLUE   BM AVON GREEN   BM MELTED ICE CREAM

BM SLIP   F&B STIFFKEY BLUE   BM CRISP LINEN   SW CHINESE RED

BM PEALE GREEN   F&B BORROWED LIGHT   SW MELLOW CORAL   C&K CONCRETE

BM: BENJAMIN MOORE · C&K: CLARK & KENSINGTON · F&B:

Picking actual COLORS for kids' rooms can be really difficult. What looks like a very pale pink on a chip can turn a room into a Pepto-Bismol nightmare once it's on the wall. Here are some of our tested favorites for kids' rooms. Bolder colors are best used as accents, while paler tones are great for entire rooms—but if you're feeling bold, GO FOR IT! It is a kid's room, after all, and paint can always be changed for very little money. And hey, some of these may work perfectly in an adult room too!

BM PINK CORSAGE   V CLASSIC LILAC   BM THORNTON SAGE   V ROYAL NAVY

BM VAN COURTLAND BLUE   C&K BEACH COTTAGE   V QUITE RED   BM CHAMBER YELLOW

FARROW & BALL · SW: SHERWIN WILLIAMS · V: VALSPAR

PARENT RETREATS

the myth of having it all

The chaos of having a baby, after trying so hard and so long for one, was oddly what I needed to finally feel at ease with much of my life, even if it was crazier than ever. It felt like I finally had everything I wanted. But even with all this newfound contentment, I really was dying to get back to work. I love being a mom and am so glad the role suits me better than I ever thought it would, but from the get-go I

OPPOSITE: In my formal living room I splurged on a luxurious sky-blue velvet sofa and a commissioned abstract piece by Kayce Hughes.

knew I would not make a good stay-at-home mom. I admire all moms equally and feel that this is such a personal decision. Some women, including close friends of mine, are very happy and successful working exclusively from home (because it IS work) at raising their children. I just knew I wasn't one of them. I waited a long time to even have a baby because I was working so hard to build a meaningful career doing what I love. I never considered giving up my career to raise children.

Of course, I am extremely fortunate to have the luxury and freedom to work for myself, so I have quite a bit of leeway when it comes to my schedule. If I want to take an afternoon off to take Henry to a museum or a birthday party, I can. Because I worked to establish my career first, I can step away and my business can keep running. Even given that freedom, I was physically back at work six weeks after giving birth (remotely only two weeks after)—much sooner than I would have been had I worked for someone else! Partially because I missed my job and NEEDED to be there (a ship can sail without a captain only so long), but also because I was craving a break from the monotony of caring for a newborn. Yes, it's beautiful and magical, but it can also be mind-numbingly boring if you're used to the crazy day-to-day stimulation of being in an office.

Another reason I went back to work is quite simply because I *had* to go back to work. Like much of the world, Andrew and I are a two-income household. Leaving my job was not an

OPPOSITE: I swapped in a raw wood chest for the black buffet that used to be here, featured on the cover of my first book, but kept a lot of the same accessories. A vintage chair I bought for ninety-five dollars was also reupholstered in a striped linen.

ABOVE: My well-loved armless leather chair is flanked by an acrylic console with a custom-upholstered storage ottoman underneath (which holds more of Henry's toys!).

ABOVE: Like our house, we have some more formal moments as a family too.

come in the door and he sees that I'm home, his huge smile and yell of "Mommy's home!" is like having Christmas morning every single day. As he grows up, I hope that having a strong, independent working woman as his (doting!) mother will influence how he views and treats women for the rest of his life.

That said, every choice in motherhood, as in life, comes with a consequence. As they say, you can't "have it all," or at least you can't have it all at the same time. For me, the consequence of being a busy working mom is that I miss a lot. I'm not there to share in Henry's developmental shifts hour to hour and day to day, attending classes with him and watching him interact with other children and adults and observing the wonder he exhibits learning new skills. I get videos and pictures during the day from my wonderful nanny, and it often pains me to see all he's doing on his own, without my being present—from learning a new dance in a class to enjoying visiting the lions at the zoo. I have a hard-and-fast rule that I am home at five p.m. every night so I can feed him dinner, give him his bath, and put him to bed. But even so, the guilt I feel can be overwhelming at times. When he cries in the morning as I am getting ready to leave for work, clinging to my leg, my heart cracks open and I feel the tears prick my eyes. He always wants to wave goodbye to me from "his" window in the

option we even considered because it would have entailed changing a lot about our lifestyle, starting with moving out of the house that I had designed to be our dream home. Luckily, I get to make a living doing some pretty cool stuff that really makes me happy and fulfilled, which is a huge part of what makes me a good mother. When I come home after working all day, I am ready to focus on Henry. When I

kitchen, perched on his little step stool. It's bittersweet to see his adorable face through the glass excitedly waving me off. Sometimes, on rougher days, I wonder if the choice I've made is the right one. But again and again I come back to the deeply rooted knowledge that the decision I've made to continue to work, which is a profoundly personal choice, is in fact the best choice for me and therefore Henry as well. I'll always believe that a happy, contented mom is the best kind of mom for any child—however that contentment is gained.

These decisions are some of the hardest women have to make in life—the decision to stop working, keep working, or go back to work are all really difficult. Most women don't even have a choice, or the flexibility I have, which is even more brutal. And unfortunately, we women are not only incredibly hard on ourselves, we are also tough on other women. I've never felt more judged by other women than I do as a mother. From the decision to breastfeed, to sleep training . . . even how I dress him—I've gotten commentary on it all. Some I asked for, some I didn't. When you're a mother, everyone feels free to weigh in— family, friends, even strangers! Once another mom at the playground asked me if I dressed Henry so nattily every day (he happened to be rocking some mighty fine duds on a Sunday morning) and when I said yes, she said, "Oh, you

must not work, then. . . . " Boy, did she know what was what by the time I left the swing set! By putting my personal experiences and life on the blog and social media, I knew that there would be criticism. And typically the underhanded and snarky comments are easy to dismiss, but no comment stings quite like the one coming from a mother as she criticizes how you choose to raise your child.

I remember being so excited to post about my design for Henry's nursery, and while most of the comments were lovely, there were some that were critical and mean. Social media makes feeling bad and behaving badly waaaaaaay too easy these days. Every day we see carefully composed highlight reels of other women's lives, many of them mothers, showcasing their perfect homes and perfect children eating perfect homemade organic acai bowls against the backdrop of a perfectly beautiful sky. It's almost impossible not to feel like a failure when you're staring at your own child chowing down on a Pop-Tart while rotting his brain in front of the TV. The anonymity that the internet affords us allows us to judge, criticize, and shame from behind a screen with no real repercussions for our words and actions. It's easy to forget that behind these profile pictures are real people—people who read those comments and take each one of them to heart.

I like to mix old and new in most rooms I design—a vintage rug and mirror from Andrew's grandparents are combined with a new sofa, abstract art, and a modern coffee table.

I try hard now not to share too much about my parenting style, which is based on intuition and not books or "techniques." Andrew and I are very laid-back parents who, yes, allow our toddler ample screen time (the horror!) and sugar (might as well be drugs!). Not everything that passes his lips is organic, and I once caught him eating snow with dog pee on it. But you know what? He's a happy, kind, lovely kid, and that's all I'm after in the long run. He may not be the biggest or the smartest. I doubt he'll be solving long-division problems at the age of four. But my sense of self-worth isn't entangled with Henry's achievements. My only concerns are that he has a strong sense of self, that he feels joy, and that he knows he is secure, safe, and deeply loved.

I am far from the perfect mother, and in no way "have it all." And there is no one "perfect motherhood experience" or guidebook to how to do it right so your kids turn out perfect and get into Harvard. Just as every child is different, every parent is different. What works for one family may seem insane to you, but think of it this way: you wouldn't assume a single pair of jeans would fit fifty totally different women, right? Each of us has a unique shape and style and age—just as we all have different children and different ways of surviving this thing called parenthood. So instead of judging and forcing our own belief systems

onto others, we should all just raise a glass of whatever the hell we want and toast ourselves and then one another for making it through another day. Because the one thing that IS universal: man, this parenting stuff is hard. And it is amazing.

OPPOSITE: I found this framed print at a small antique shop and it turns out it's a Picasso lithograph! I love leaning it against the new mirror above our fireplace.

ABOVE: Our see-through fireplace connects the new family room with the formal living room, creating a nice flow when entertaining.

FORMAL LIVING ROOMS

Many homes these days don't have a formal living room. Maybe it's now a playroom, or perhaps there wasn't one to begin with—some builders aren't even bothering to put a formal living room in at all and instead create extra-large family rooms. But if you DO have one, it's lovely to make a special spot to spend time with your significant other when the day is done or alone with a glass of wine and a magazine when you need a little "me time." The formal living spaces of today don't convey the old uptight feel that you really shouldn't sit down on anything. Your living room can be a space that is a little more tailored, filled with fine, pretty things—one in which you feel like a real, live grown-up.

OPPOSITE: This grand formal living room features back-to-back sofas to best make use of the long, narrow space.

PLAN OUT YOUR SEATING

Typically, in formal living rooms we avoid using a sectional and instead choose sofas (alone or in pairs) and accent chairs. Think about how you like to entertain and how people seem to flow in the room. If you have a fireplace, we always like to have the seating arranged with that as the focal point. If not, you can create a focal point with a large chest with statement art above or something tall like an armoire.

THE BEST WHITES

White paint may seem easy, but it's not! When looking for a trim, cabinet, or wall color there are so many whites to choose from that it can be incredibly daunting. Our rule of thumb is to pick a white that coordinates with your home style and surrounding colors—if your home is more traditional and has more warm tones, pick a white with a slight creamy undertone. If it's more modern or simple, try a white with a more blue-gray undertone.

BM SIMPLY WHITE   SW GREEK VILLA   BM CHANTILLY LACE   BM WHITE DOVE

F&B GREAT WHITE   B NIGHT BLOOMING JASMINE   BM DECORATOR'S WHITE   SW EXTRA WHITE

B: BEHR   ·   BM: BENJAMIN MOORE   ·   F&B: FARROW & BALL
SW: SHERWIN-WILLIAMS

A BEVY OF TABLES

Since entertaining is a big part of a formal living room's function, I always like to think about where every person in every seat will want to put down their drink. We use lots of cute smaller "drink drop" tables for this reason—either between chairs or paired with each chair, as well as side tables and cocktail tables. Many times we also will place a smaller game table with a pair of chairs in a formal living room as a place to eat or simply play a game. I prefer to use a mix of metal, glass, wood, and stone tables but have one unifying feature tie them together—like a metal finish. And I also try to mix up the shapes—too many rounds or squares can feel repetitive.

ABOVE: A natural grass cloth warms up the walls of this formal living room that has French doors leading into an elegant wood-paneled office.

ABOVE: A low modern coffee table and various types of seating provide an ideal setup for hosting a cocktail party. Design by Ashley Garelick.

LEFT: Coffee table accessories add color and texture.

OPPOSITE, TOP TO BOTTOM: In this space by Ashley Garelick the views are the star, with the sectional and fabrics complementing the tones found in the landscape. ❙ Jenn Feldman masterfully mixes color with neutrals in this open, airy formal living room in California. The extra-large scale of the coffee table is perfectly balanced by the oversized sofa. Emerald lamps add a touch of cool color to the warmer palette.

OPPOSITE: We designed this suburban living room with a base of neutrals but big, bright accents of blue and magenta. A favorite lamp by Bunny Williams makes an artistic statement.

ABOVE: A smaller vintage blue rug layered over a room-size jute anchors the furniture. A pair of glass and brass étagères frame the far window and provide some height to the space.

RIGHT: The combination of a traditional chest with a modern painting and antique primitive sculpture is such a winning combination.

ABOVE: Our clients wanted their formal living room to be a sanctuary for them that felt more "California modern" than the rest of their traditional New England home.

LEFT: Brass lighting and accents mirror the brass base of the modern taupe leather chair. The linear stone mantel is modern and yet based in tradition.

OPPOSITE: A pair of wide-striped chairs sit in front of custom paisley fabric draperies and welcome you into this soothing space.

ABOVE: We incorporated some of the home-owner's beloved antiques into our design for this charming living room.

OPPOSITE: In this coastal home we used blue trim on tall draperies to emphasize the large windows and then brought that color in through pillows and lamps as well.

WHAT CLICHÉ/OUTDATED ADVICE DO YOU WISH PEOPLE WOULD STOP LISTENING TO WHEN IT COMES TO DECORATING A FAMILY HOME?

That everything needs to be kid friendly and/or pristine. I use a lot of vintage and antique furniture because of the inherent character that shows from years of living with these pieces. The imperfection is what makes things feel interesting: water rings, time-worn finishes, etc. Let's stop freaking out about letting our kids around the things we love.

—NATE BERKUS
INTERIOR DESIGNER AND AUTHOR

STATEMENT ART

When the budget allows, I always like to include some original and dramatic art in a formal living room. Again, since this is a space more dedicated to the older folks of the house, you can stretch your imagination a little further when it comes to the decorative items. I commissioned an amazing painting for my formal living room (once we had one, thanks to our new family room) and, even though the space serves more as a pass-through for us right now, walking by that painting over my fun blue sofa makes me smile every day. And you really should have an item or two in your home that does that for you too!

OPPOSITE: This living room is extremely long and narrow, so we paired back-to-back loveseats with a console in between to create two seating areas for the homeowners to entertain in and added a special piece of art above the fireplace to draw the eye.

ABOVE: Simple drapery panels frame the expansive windows and a custom grass-cloth-wrapped table was made extra large to fill the space properly.

ABOVE: A pair of existing wingbacks flank a fireplace, while a zebra ottoman and beautiful landscape painting add interest and color to the cozy seating area.

ABOVE: Farmhouse style doesn't have to mean casual—this room by Nikki Dalrymple exudes a laid-back vibe but a touch of modern sensibility too. The life-size sheep sculpture proves art doesn't always have to hang on your walls.

RIGHT: Patterned tile, like Nikki Dalrymple used here, can make for an interesting fireplace surround when done in rustic materials.

ABOVE: I love creating multiple seating areas within larger rooms, like this pair of wingbacks around a round side table large enough to play a game on or use for appetizers.

LEFT: The back of this sofa faces the entrance to the formal living room, so we finished it off with an open console full of fun accessories and books.

OPPOSITE: This gold bookcase came from the client's former condo and worked beautifully in the space when filled with her collection of blue-and-white ceramics and books.

OPPOSITE, TOP: Pulling the orange from the Hermès scarf framed on the wall, we added accents of the color in other places throughout the room. Overscale chevron-print drapes are neutral but unique.

OPPOSITE, BOTTOM LEFT TO RIGHT: We fell madly in love with this framed Hermès scarf our client had, so we made it the focal point of the living room bar area. ▌ Layering various styles of art—photography, drawings, and abstracts—within one space creates an interesting and complementary look.

ABOVE: Our client has a passion for riding, so we made this amazing photograph our jumping-off point for the room. A burled wood coffee table and accents of brown and tan complement the horse's beautiful coat.

OPPOSITE: Painting the interior of a built-in cabinet a dark and moody navy allows the accessories stored in there to really pop. Design by KidderKokx Interior Architecture & Design.

ABOVE: This living room features a magnificent mural paper (the same one as in Henry's nursery, actually) that acts as large-scale art!

ABOVE: Charming pen-and-ink drawings of her children look beautiful and elegant in photographer Sarah Winchester's living room.

OPPOSITE: In the same living room, a pair of traditional tufted Chesterfield sofas mix beautifully with a modern chandelier and artwork by Sarah Winchester herself.

ABOVE: We designed this living room as a comfortable but refined space that mixes traditional elements with modern sensibility.

OPPOSITE: Our clients were nervous about this sleek chair done in a bright green velvet being too modern for them, but it is now one of their favorite parts of the room!

ABOVE: Designer Alison Sheffield knocked it out of the park by wallpapering her entire living room in this neutral zebra wallpaper and combining it with a red Heriz-style vintage rug.

OPPOSITE: The dark chocolate walls of the dining room, seen through the doorway, pick up on the tones of the wingback chairs, uniting the formal living and dining spaces of designer Alison Sheffield's home.

BOTTOMS UP

When the stress of parenting makes me feel like jumping off a cliff, it's nice to know I can turn to a dependable parenting aid—booze. So creating a bar (either a dedicated space or just a cart) is a great addition to a formal dining or living area. A lot of times we build this kind of space within a butler's pantry, with a wine fridge, wine racks, and sometimes even a custom kegerator! Have some fun in here, with a bolder backsplash tile or cabinet color or search for a cool vintage bar cart that will add some serious style to your living space.

OPPOSITE: A small bar cart can be tucked into a corner and brought out for entertaining.

ABOVE: This client had a wonderful collection of small landscape paintings purchased over the years—we hung smaller gallery walls flanking a large window to show them off!

OPPOSITE: When renovating their kitchen, our clients decided they wanted a glamorous bar area in the pass-through between the kitchen and formal living room. We used high-gloss deep-gray cabinetry and lots of brass details to create just that.

ABOVE: In this butler's pantry, we chose a show-stopping patterned marble tile as a backsplash and painted the cabinetry a rich gray. The hardware is custom-made with shagreen-wrapped handles.

ABOVE, LEFT TO RIGHT: In this butler's pantry/bar area we used a patterned grass-cloth paper to unite the wood countertops and white cabinetry. ▌ Designer Jenn Feldman placed a traditional bar car in front of a massive abstract canvas to create a real "moment" within a living space.

ABOVE, LEFT TO RIGHT: Fine cabinetry details and a glossy lacquer paint job make for a jaw-droppingly glamorous bar by Patricia Knox. ❙ Designer Alison Sheffield perked up an existing bar area by painting the cabinetry navy and installing a bold patterned paper as a backdrop.

DINING ROOMS

While the formal living room is disappearing, the formal dining room is not. It may not get the most use of all the rooms in the house, but people still really want to have a nice space in their home to host holiday or celebratory dinners or simply a fun dinner party. It's nice to have more elegant meals once in a while, not only for yourself but for your children too—manners are an important skill to impart, of course. We don't want to end up with twenty-two-year-olds who think it's okay to sit cross-legged and eat with their hands, do we?

OPPOSITE: In one of my favorite dining rooms I've ever designed we wrapped the room in a custom mural paper by Susan Harter and paired the custom dining table with moss-green Louis-style chairs and a super-modern chandelier.

MODERNIZING HAND-ME-DOWNS

For a long time, our dining table and chairs were an antique set gifted to us when Andrew's grandparents moved to the South. It wasn't my style at the time, so I painted the shield-back chairs bright white and reupholstered the seats in a zebra linen. And for a long time I actually LOVED how it all looked. These days, our clients often want to work with an existing hand-me-down dining table for sentimental or budgetary reasons (not to mention, older goods are usually better made!). The best way to modernize an old-fashioned table is to use modern, updated chairs with it. People will barely notice the table if you have it surrounded with funky, cool chairs or older ones upholstered in a bold, modern fabric. If the table is ornate, keep the lines of the chairs clean and simple, and if the table is simple, try some more intricately styled chairs. You may find yourself not wanting to replace your dining table after all!

ABOVE: We made roman shades out of a taupe silk with a graphic border and used the same fabric for sconce shades on the vintage fixtures.

OPPOSITE: To offset the traditional mural we chose an abstract painting by Mallory Page for above the wood-burning fireplace.

TEXTURE & TEXTILES

While we rarely use a rug under casual dining tables, we do use them under formal dining tables. Nothing cozies up a room like a great rug, especially when most of the furniture is hard and not upholstered. A well-worn vintage Persian will hide any rogue wine stains resulting from that intense political debate you had with your stodgy uncle last Thanksgiving. Another great way to add some warmth to the dining room is grass-cloth wallcovering (in case you haven't noticed, grass cloth is one of my favorites!). Used in a deeper color, it can add a much more cozy, romantic vibe than paint alone.

OPPOSITE, LEFT TO RIGHT: We had a contemporary buffet made in the same wood tone as the dining table but with sleek white door fronts and oversize brass hardware. ❙ We repeated the host-chair fabric as roman shades and added drapes with graphic trim to give the room a luxe, layered feel. The vintage rug is a perfectly muted complement.

ABOVE: This existing dining room set was made new again by reupholstering the side chairs and incorporating new host chairs done in a modern fabric. The walls are covered in a taupe grass cloth.

ABOVE, LEFT TO RIGHT: Kate Coughlin's deep plum and turquoise palette for this dining room is such a fabulous study in how to use saturated colors in a truly elegant way. ❙ The multicolor drapery panels and two-tone upholstered chairs blend colors together in a balanced and tasteful way in this bold room.

ABOVE, LEFT TO RIGHT: We installed navy grass cloth in this dining room and used a wide, graphic trim on the ivory drapes to keep the room from getting too dark. An edgy chandelier keeps the otherwise traditional room from feeling too "old." ❙ We upholstered these Louis-style chairs in a durable small-diamond fabric, which makes them feel crisp.

ABOVE: We chose a blue-gray paint color for the tray ceiling in the dining room that matches the patterned grass-cloth wallcoverings to draw attention to the architectural detail.

ABOVE: A mix of finishes, both traditional in nature and modern in material, help create a truly interesting space.

LOCATING THE LIGHT

A rule of thumb we designers use is to always have the bottom of the dining room light fixture thirty inches above the top of the table. If it's a little higher that's okay, but if it's too high it feels less formal and intimate, and if it's lower, your guests will have trouble talking to each other and you will be limited in your table décor, especially flowers.

OPPOSITE: Tones of peacock blue and crisp white mix perfectly with dark wood and brass in this formal dining room, which mixes affordable finds with custom detailing.

ABOVE, LEFT TO RIGHT: A modern art print works well with a pair of traditional blue-and-white lamps and blue wallpaper. ▌ A pretty table setting for a dinner party.

OPPOSITE: We reupholstered the chairs of this midcentury dining set with a fun woven fabric that matched the tribal carpet perfectly, but the ornate yet contemporary light fixture is the real star of the space.

ABOVE: Using a modern riveted paper on the walls of this dining room by Jenn Feldman makes the more traditional furniture feel youthful.

ABOVE, LEFT TO RIGHT: This monochromatic dining room is a great example of how to combine wood finishes well and use pattern, rather than color, in big ways to create interest. ❚ When you have a room with gorgeous iron windows, you don't want to cover them up! Designer Julie Richard instead used strong pops of blue to create drama and depth.

ABOVE: A love of blue is evident in this dining room, where we paired a freshly painted antique hutch with large-scale patterned drapes and soft-blue velvet chairs. The walls are a vinyl grass cloth.

ABOVE: We added tape trim to the skirts of a pair of store-bought host chairs to make them feel more custom and connect them to the gray faux-bamboo side chairs. An acrylic-and-nickel fixture adds a modern touch.

ABOVE: Colleen Simonds's dining room features a bright combination of modern orange chairs paired with a streamlined wood farm table.

ENTRIES
& POWDER
ROOMS

As I've said before (and will say again), the formal entry to your home should act as a welcoming space that introduces your visitors to your style. While some people have grand spaces to work with, others (like myself) have barely any. Either way you can make the entry you DO have into something that feels unique and reflective of your personal style. Maybe it's a single wall of statement wallpaper or a great storage bench that also functions as a place to stash shoes—thoughtful and personal touches that are both beautiful and functional are key in this space.

OPPOSITE: The entry to this historical home has great bones, so we simply added a subtle patterned paper and vintage console to the mix.

AN INTRODUCTORY VIGNETTE

At my firm, we seem to have a bit of a formula when it comes to entry décor. Given a slightly grander space, we love to use a console with benches below it or a chest with a chair or two beside it. On top, we want a light fixture or two and a large mirror or sometimes a piece of art. A great rug typically welcomes our clients into their home as well. With different-size spaces, we adjust this formula to fit the scale—sometimes it's a tiny console and a basket, or simply some wall hooks and a bench! Whatever the combination is, be sure to have good light, a place to put something down, and an element that really speaks to your style and what you love (art, fabric, wallpaper—anything!).

ABOVE, LEFT TO RIGHT: Panels of framed scenic wallpaper are a great option for creating impact that you can take with you when you move! ❙ A traditional but not stuffy entry vignette featuring a gorgeous custom-made chest.

The entry in this modern condo is tight but big on style—an open-ribbed console and x-benches provide seating and storage but don't block the intricate railing details. A photograph by Michael Gaillard of Nantucket reminds the family of a beloved vacation spot.

ABOVE, LEFT TO RIGHT: A small monochromatic gallery wall welcomes you into photographer Sarah Winchester's home. ▌ A linen-wrapped double dresser provides extra storage and ample countertop space to drop keys and mail.

ABOVE: I found these incredible painted chairs in an antique shop and they create a special pop of color in this entryway in combination with the blue-and-white pottery collection.

THE STAIRS HAVE IT

In my entry, as you may have seen before, you walk right into the stairs. Almost literally. So I made those stairs the star of the show by using a bold-leopard-print stair runner, which has now become sort of my calling card. And up the stairs I hung a gallery wall of family photos, art, and small mirrors. While there isn't a square inch to spare, when people come in the house they are greeted by something that totally shows off our style. If you plan on installing a runner up your front stairs, consider going bold! It hides a lot of dirt and wear and tear (my cut-pile wool is like iron!). Another way to dress up the stairway is to wallpaper the wall, perfect when working with a narrow space as you don't need art or other items to accessorize (and fall off the wall when you are running up the stairs for the twenty-eighth time looking for someone's lost shoe).

CLOCKWISE, FROM ABOVE: With busy (and messy) kids afoot, Sarah Winchester chose an indoor-outdoor version of this popular antelope carpet for her stairs, and it has worn like iron! ❙ Stair runners help our furry friends and kids get up and down comfortably and safely. ❙ A set of stairs is transformed into a dramatic artistic moment through graphic mural-style wallpaper. Design by Jessie Miller.

OPPOSITE: As you know from my first book, I have almost zero entry, so using a bold leopard carpet on the stairs was my opportunity for a style statement. I incorporated some of Henry's art into the gallery wall too!

ABOVE: This large open landing needed some furniture to warm it up, so we added a long tufted bench and some colorful pillows in addition to a statement lantern.

LEFT: A huge giclée print is an important addition to this winding hallway, as it takes the space from boring to impactful.

OPPOSITE: We wallpapered the long stairwell wall in this entry in a subtle organic paper and used a geometric outdoor fabric to top a storage bench.

AN EASY TRANSITION

A lot of people aren't sure how to handle the transition from the stairwell to the upstairs hallway when implementing wallpaper and rugs. We recommend two approaches: either go big and use the same rug and/or wallpaper throughout both the stairway and hallway (the pricier option), or you can accent just the stairs or a single wall going up the stairs with something bold and fun and then use a solid paint color or solid carpet to do the hallway areas, which will save you money but still allow for an impactful lower-level entry.

DON'T IGNORE THE HALLWAYS

You may have design fatigue by the time you have to deal with private hallways on your upper floor, but put in a little effort and come up with something pretty to make this passageway pretty! If you have a window seat, use some fun, bold pillows to dress it up or install a gallery wall of family pictures or a large, funky piece of art!

THE POWER OF THE POWDER

The powder room is one of my FAVORITE rooms to design in a home because people always want to have more fun and make more daring choices in these small rooms. Sometimes it even leads them to branch out and be bolder in larger, more public rooms of the house too! Our favorite element of a powder room is always wallpaper. Big and bold or soft and ethereal, a patterned wall will add interest to the small room, make it feel more grand, and create a unique statement personal to your home.

OPPOSITE: A spunky chartreuse-and-gray wallpaper is exactly the facelift this powder room needed. The brass mirror and sculptural sconces are icing on the cake!

ABOVE, LEFT TO RIGHT: This powder room is minuscule, so we covered it in a small hexagon pattern, which helps trick the eye into thinking it's a bit bigger! ▮ A stark ocean photograph floats over the busy graphic wallpaper and breaks it up.

ABOVE, LEFT TO RIGHT: Navy zebra paper is a classic (but bold) choice. Brass accents contrast perfectly with the navy shade and pop off the paper. ▌ A modern wood vanity with marble top is warmed up by this leafy paper done in similar tones. The mirror was made from frame molding to fit the space perfectly.

OPPOSITE: A chic and stunning glass-legged console sink blends in with this pale neutral leafy paper gracefully.

OPPOSITE: Powder rooms are the perfect place to use a wallpaper you may find too overwhelming for a larger space, like this Asian-influenced design. A big abstract print gives the eye a place to rest.

LEFT: Small-scale papers like this one are a comfortable and casual way to dress up a less formal powder room. The rope mirror adds to the farmhouse appeal.

A STATEMENT SINK

Since there aren't a whole lot of supplies you need to store in a powder room, it's often a place to use a pretty pedestal or console-style sink. These sinks help a small room feel larger and offer up a little bit of a more glamorous look. And if you need storage, baskets or even a small étagère work wonders for extra toilet paper, towels, and the like. If you want to go a step further, you can have a tradesman retrofit an antique dresser or console into a sink for you— then you have not only a statement piece but one that also provides storage.

ABOVE, LEFT TO RIGHT: A grass-cloth-wrapped mirror adds texture atop the blockprint-style paper here. ▎ Because we didn't use a vanity in this bath, we chose a metal-and-glass cabinet to store extra toilet paper and towels.

CLOCKWISE, FROM ABOVE: A large-scale gray-and-white paper mimics the tones found in the beautiful marble sink atop a console base in this classically beautiful powder room. ❙ This gorgeous sink was carved from a single piece of marble. ❙ Retrofitting an antique console or dresser to act as a vanity is a great way to create a truly inimitable look in a powder room—especially when combined with fun wallpaper. Design by Alison Sheffield.

LEFT: A warm wood vanity with faux-bamboo detailing isn't the only interesting thing in this powder room by Patricia Knox—the blue floor tile, patterned grass cloth, and shell-patterned mirror all contribute to the overall glamour.

OPPOSITE: Dark blue paneling below block-printed bird and branch wallpaper hums in unison with a light-blue vanity, making this powder room by Emily Butler a very special spot.

FANCY FINISHES

As opposed to other bathrooms in your home, the powder room will get more face time with guests, so make sure the finishes and fixtures in there are up to snuff! Many clients will try a new finish in the powder room—brass, for example—when they like it but are too afraid to commit to it in a larger room. Install decent lighting and have nice hand towels out that people can actually USE. No fancy pressed linen that leaves people scared to dry their hands!

ABOVE, LEFT TO RIGHT: Jenn Feldman used the black-and-white version of Schumacher's famed Chiang Mai Dragon wallpaper to turn this powder room into a graphic statement. ❚ When kids have access to the powder room, we like to use beadboard chair rail to shield the walls from splashes, which allows you to use fancy paper where it's safe!

ABOVE: A tile-patterned wallpaper envelops you as you enter this elegant powder room by Kate Coughlin.

MASTER SUITES

O ne of my favorite rooms in my house is my master suite. We built this addition in 2015 (right before Henry's birth), and while we had some limitations with size and shape, I was basically able to create the bedroom of my dreams: tons of windows, high ceilings, a built-in window seat, huge canopy bed, and gorgeous master bathroom. I still love retreating to this room at the end of each day; it's totally my happy place. I am even happier to have it now that I'm a mom. When Henry was an infant, it gave us ample room for his bassinet, and since I broke the cardinal rule of "no TV in the bedroom" and slapped a big ol' flat-screen across from my bed, it was the most heavenly place in which to recuperate from giving birth. Lots of great, snuggly memories were made there during the early months. These days, it's

OPPOSITE: I kept the palette neutral but selected a paisley-patterned fabric for the drapes in my master bedroom to make a statement.

my sanctuary after a long day of work and trying to convince a screaming Henry to go to bed. And it's where Andrew and I have mini date nights, snuggling up to watch a movie or TV show in the evening (because finding a sitter can be really tough!). The one thing that's missing is a nice freestanding tub, but hey, a girl has to have dreams, right?

In my short time as a mom, I can tell you parenthood does a number on your relationship too. Andrew and I are both working full-time, and in the minimal time we have together on nights and weekends we focus primarily on Henry, leaving very limited time for just "us." The other day Andrew looked at me and said, "Can you even remember a time when it was just the two of us?" Between the dogs (who are sometimes more work than Henry) and a child, it's so hard to imagine just what we DID with all that free time! Right now we maybe have a "date night" once every couple months, and more often

---

ABOVE, LEFT TO RIGHT: This window seat offers hidden storage for off-season bedding and provides a perfect perch for the dogs and Henry to enjoy. ❙ The TV is a necessary evil, but I really love bingeing on Netflix in bed as a way to relax, so here it is—above a grass-cloth-wrapped dresser topped with interesting accents.

are found in bed watching another Netflix series before passing out cold by 9:30 p.m.! Romantic it's not, but we have a strong relationship and know that we are knee-deep in the crazy years, the time of life where we just don't have the leisure of gazing into each other's eyes and planning a romantic jaunt to Italy. We are more likely to be downing wine while shoveling Italian food in our mouths in an effort to get bathtime done at a reasonable hour! Ooh la la.

I do know we need to make time for us as a couple so the strong relationship I mentioned stays that way. Since we are both gone all day during the week, we want to spend as much time as we can with Henry when we're home, so that seems to take precedence over going to see a movie or out to dinner. Guilt supersedes everything in parenthood, after all! However, I know that if we keep brushing "us" aside and waiting for our kid to grow older to find time for each other, then it may become a habit that is tough to break. So we talk a lot about how to

ABOVE, LEFT TO RIGHT: The long entry hall to our new master features an accent wall with wallpaper and antique sconces and a vintage rug sourced from Etsy. **I** We stole a little space from the adjoining bedroom to create a long wall of closets and drawers for Andrew in the entry hallway as well as a bookcase. **I** A vintage candle sconce I picked up in Palm Beach.

make a bigger, better effort at having "alone" time and alleviating the guilt that comes along with that. But in the meantime, we're just so damn tired at the end of the day that an hour watching TV in bed in our beautiful bedroom sounds like way more fun than putting on heels and looking for parking in the city!

I've noticed in my time designing for families that the master bedroom is often last or near last on the list. Not to stereotype, but I suspect this comes from women innately putting themselves last (and a lot of men I work with not caring as much about design). Take my word for it: it's SO important to have a space for yourself, especially a calming and relaxing place to sleep and unwind. You deserve it.

OPPOSITE, LEFT TO RIGHT: My walk-in closet is tiny, but I made it feel grand with a custom sheer roman shade, built-in hamper, and vintage rug. ❚ Using a custom closet company helped me utilize every inch of my small closet smartly.

ABOVE: I designed my four-poster bed with a white faux-leather headboard to emphasize the height in the room. The walls and ceiling are painted Sherwin-Williams Incredible White.

OPPOSITE: This master suite is resplendent in tones of cream, beige, and pale aqua.

LEFT: These roman shades, featuring chevron trim, frame the windows perfectly. A pale-aqua slipcovered chair is the perfect spot to relax with a good book.

GET SOME SHUT-EYE

Just as proper drapes are essential to nurseries and kids' rooms, so too are they for your room. Sleep may not come in massive quantities once you become a parent, so focus on its quality. A nice dark bedroom is essential for this. In my room, I layered woven wood shades with blackout-lined drapes and roman shades. When closed, they really block out everything from light to noise to drafts. Many retailers now offer blackout lining as an option for their drapes too, so it's not something only reserved for those who have the budget for custom goods.

ABOVE: Shades of gray, linen, and white create a soothing and traditional master bedroom featuring a small entry papered in a paisley print and original floral sketches.

LEFT: A Swedish-inspired chest of drawers and block-print roman shade mix new and old together in this master bedroom.

ABOVE: We ditched the matching nightstands from this existing bedroom set in favor of a modern contrasting pair and added a metal-frame bench, instantly updating the look of this traditional bed.

RIGHT: A long built-in window seat is dressed up in custom pillows and topped with an abstract-print roman shade. We made upholstered framed panels that fit right into the curved window above for nighttime!

LEFT: We upholstered this chair in a small-chevron woven fabric and gave it a punch of chartreuse through a custom pillow trimmed in a stripe piping.

OPPOSITE: This suite is actually a guest space, so it was a fun room to go wild with color through chartreuse and aqua paper and accents, including a painted tray ceiling.

A PALETTE FOR CALM

I tend to like to keep master bedrooms rather neutral and light. Bold colors can be a bit too energizing for inducing sleep, so save those for accents if you want to use them. But find ways to make a softer palette interesting by playing with texture—grass cloth or patterned wallpaper, thick rugs, tufted furniture, soft upholstered pieces (I love using velvet for headboards), and rich draperies.

A NONMATCHY MASTER

When a bed has wood and fabric, it's fine to use a matching nightstand to avoid too many mixed finishes. But change up the material for the dresser—like this linen upholstered one!

 +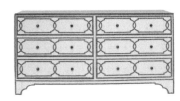

We will use matching nightstands and dressers on occasion, but then make sure the bed is very different—like this fully upholstered platform bed with nailhead trim. Simple yet glamourous.

 +

You CAN make three different finishes look cohesive—this painted black bed looks great paired with simple antique-inspired wood side tables. A grass-cloth-wrapped dresser rounds it out with some texture and clean lines.

 +

One thing I typically try to avoid in a master bedroom is buying bedroom "sets." Sometimes I'll use a pair of items from a set (say a bed and a dresser) but mix in a different nightstand. This helps make the space seem unique and different from a page in a catalog.

A patterned headboard pairs nicely with a solid painted-finish nightstand with strong lines. To add some movement, consider a chest with an ornate wood-grain pattern. Masculine yet refined.

This dark-iron canopy bed works well with a black nightstand, which complements the metal finish of the bed. The same metal is then repeated in the hardware on the wood dresser, which really unifies everything.

An antique-inspired wood-framed headboard looks lovely with this Swedish-inspired painted dresser with vintage brass hardware. In this case, the best nightstand is a simple brass table with antiqued glass.

LEFT: A modern four-poster bed adds a little bit of drama to this otherwise calming master bedroom.

ABOVE, LEFT TO RIGHT: In the entry to the room we used a soft paisley-patterned paper to add a little significance to the pass-through space. ▌ Crisp white side tables and pale sea-green lamps sit underneath a window topped with a custom roman shade with detailed tape trim.

OPPOSITE: This sea-glass-colored fabric on the wingback chair was chosen to complement the gorgeous ocean photograph we procured for above the fireplace.

OPPOSITE: Colleen Simonds brilliantly mixes patterns in this ice-blue master bedroom.

LEFT: A wood dresser resonates with the wood beam above it while the velvet chair adds softness and a rich dose of color.

BEDDING BASICS

Andrew likes to joke that we have disposable bedding. Our two dogs sleep in bed with us and so between them, my penchant for self-tanner, and Henry snuggle time, our bright white duvets and shams really take a beating. But I really don't like anything but white bedding, so we've just had to invest in bleach and deal. The good news is, you don't need to spend a fortune to get nice bedding. Thread count isn't the most important thing—that's one of the myths I'd like to dispel. The quality of the material and manufacturing are more important in creating a beautiful-feeling and -looking product. I like to order retail-store bedding and have a custom monogram added. It makes it look far more expensive than it is.

ABOVE: Rich wood tones, a woven rope chair, and crisp white accents lend a bohemian influence to this otherwise traditional space.

ABOVE: We added subtle accents of color to this otherwise neutral bedroom through a custom lumbar pillow and vintage rug.

MONOGRAM GUIDE

Cece DuPraz is my local go-to for monogramming bedding (or napkins or pretty much anything that doesn't move). So I asked them to share their monogram advice for those still confused by which letter goes where and what to do if you have four names, like Henry and Andrew do!

SINGLE PERSON - THREE NAMES

ERIN TUBRIDY GATES

WHEN ALL INITIALS
ARE THE SAME SIZE

WHEN CENTER INITIAL
IS LARGER

STACKED

SINGLE PERSON - FOUR NAMES

ANDREW BRADLEY STEPHENSON GATES

HENRY FLYNN STEPHENSON GATES

WHEN ALL INITIALS
ARE THE SAME SIZE

WHEN CENTER INITIAL
IS LARGER

WHEN CENTER INITIAL
IS LARGER

STACKED

MARRIED COUPLE

ERIN AND ANDREW GATES

WHEN CENTER INITIAL IS LARGER

wife's first name | married/last name |
husband's first name

STACKED

wife's first name above | husband's first
name below | adjacent last name

INTERLOCKING

with couple's first names

HYPHENATED

with couple's first names and
hyphenated last name

In my previous master, now a guest room, I wanted a soothing combination of pale green (Farrow & Ball's Cromarty) and linen tones. The antique etchings I found at the Brimfield Antique Show and the side tables were hand-me-downs I spray-painted white.

ABOVE: The unexpected combination of pale blue and bright red looks so crisp and fun in this bedroom by Emily Butler.

ABOVE, LEFT TO RIGHT: A mix of warm and cool tones in this suite feels uplifting, and the glass lamp doesn't block any light in front of the window. ❙ A pair of coral Amanda Stone Talley paintings look eye-catching atop the gray grass cloth in this bedroom. The rug is a vintage beauty that brings all the colors together.

A MASTER BATHROOM
THAT WOWS

My master bathroom is pretty small and a slightly awkward long and narrow shape. But by using luxurious materials, like my gorgeous marble chevron floor and bold brass fixtures, I made a rather small space feel pretty grand. When working in a smaller space, you can use higher-end materials since you need so much less.

OPPOSITE: My bathroom is long and narrow but chock-full of style. The vanity is painted Benjamin Moore Chelsea Gray and the floor is a chevron marble tile.

ABOVE, LEFT TO RIGHT: A slightly beveled subway tile with darker gray grout is a subtle backdrop to the bold gold plumbing fixtures. ❙ I absolutely love my decision to use brass accents in my bathroom—it looks so rich.

DO WHAT YOU LOVE

A lot of people worry about resale value when renovating their homes. While it's wise to take this into consideration when making big decisions, I still think you have to make room for what YOU love. In my master bathroom I really wanted to use matte gold plumbing fixtures. Our real estate agent tried to talk me out of going for gold, finding it "too trendy" for resale. Well, I went ahead with my scheme and it's one of the most-commented-on features of the space now. I love it (and so does she). I don't regret it one bit.

OPPOSITE: A patterned roman shade offers privacy when using the big soaking tub in this master bathroom.

ABOVE, LEFT TO RIGHT: You can never go wrong with classic, timeless choices like polished-nickel faucets and sconces in the bathroom. ❚ This traditional runner warms up a marble floor and leads right to the massive dual-sided shower.

ABOVE: We created a separate makeup vanity in the same materials as the main vanity in this large bathroom, giving everyone room to get ready.

ABOVE, LEFT TO RIGHT: A simple and crisp window sheer and herringbone marble floors make this a refreshing spot for relaxation. ❚ Instead of replacing the plate-glass mirror, we framed it and added decorative sconces on top.

PRIORITIZE FUNCTION OVER ALL ELSE

Some people can fit everything they dream of into a master bathroom or bedroom; most of us have to pick and choose. While my bedroom allowed me pretty generous parameters within which to work, my bathroom was another story. While I would have loved a soaking tub, I knew a double vanity was more important for my day-to-day life, as well as a nice, spacious walk-in shower. A tub was a luxury we did not have space for. So I made both those features as wonderful as I could, and I'll save the freestanding soaking tub for my next house.

ABOVE, LEFT TO RIGHT: Highlighting one wall with a bold wallpaper, especially in a smaller room, may be all you need to make your bedroom feel special. **I** This five-inch-wide trim makes a set of plain white draperies look anything but simple.

OPPOSITE: Carving out little nooks, like this vanity in a hallway area of a master suite, is a great use of space. Especially when dressed up with a punchy zebra stool.

OFFICES
& DENS

W hile I personally don't have a den or home office, I did work from an extra bedroom that I had fashioned into an office when I started my company. It's funny to look back on that space now, with its kiwi-green walls and all IKEA furniture, but at the time I wanted an energizing bright space with all-white, simple furniture. That bold palette inspired my creativity and energy. Having designed many, many offices and dens since then, I have a slightly more mature perspective on what makes a functional yet inspiring space. For me, it's now a simple, neutral color scheme with as much attractive storage as I can manage! For other clients it's a darker dramatic space with texture and glamorous details. When it comes to dens, some clients want them to have dual function (as an extra guest

OPPOSITE: This wood-paneled formal office features a pair of cozy velvet swivel chairs and art hung on the bookcase to break up the business of the packed shelves.

Ivory roman shades brighten up the expanse of wood in this library, while the vintage Heriz rug and patterned ottoman add texture and pattern.

space AND home office in one) while others want it to be an escape where they can hunker down with their iPad and catch up on magazines in peace. What's most important in having these spaces be successful is to know your desires and needs from the outset and make sure those boxes are being checked while also creating an aesthetically pleasing space.

ABOVE: An antique barrister's desk looks anything but stuffy when topped with a modern lamp. The ivory drapes add a sense of airiness to the dark space.

OPPOSITE: A chambray-colored grass cloth is a cool contrast to the warm, shaggy rug in this office. The abstract prints make the room feel less serious.

OPPOSITE: A graphic Stark carpet and deep-chocolate paint create a dynamic base for the colorful patterned ottoman and wingback chair.

ABOVE: This office is separated from the living room by French doors, so we repeated the orange pillow fabric on the desk chair and the window shades to make sure the rooms felt connected.

CREATING A HOME OFFICE
CONDUCIVE TO WORKING

Working from home can be challenging. It can be hard to stay focused and productive when you know just one room over is a comfy sofa, a yummy snack, and *Ellen* on TV! I battled this when I used to work out of my home, but trust me: creating a dedicated space (even if it's not a whole room) makes work less boring and uninspiring so that you can actually improve your productivity.

ABOVE: This modern built-in painted top to bottom in a deep blue showcases the books and objects it holds. The leather chair adds a nice dose of warmth. Design by Julie Richard.

OPPOSITE, CLOCKWISE FROM TOP: This client's love of blue gave us the freedom to use it in a big way through patterned drapes and a pair of navy wingback chairs in this mom's retreat. ❚ This desk was built into the wall and includes a pinboard and cabinetry with show-stopping hardware. ❚ The vinyl grass cloth on the walls means no worries about kids running through this open office space.

CONCEAL &
CONTROL THE CLUTTER

Whether it's a desk or a whole room, when it comes to your workstation you
need to create a system that works for you. If you need a lot of file storage for
paperwork, invest in attractive filing cabinet pieces (yes, they exist). If you
prefer to see everything at once, buy yourself some great desktop trays and
accessories. Most importantly, make sure your desk has enough storage. A
leggy desk is sexy, but if you don't have a spot for a pencil or a power cord, it
quickly becomes dowdy.

OPPOSITE: This client wanted a special room all to herself in tones of blue and lilac, so we created a comfy retreat with striped swivel chairs, floral roman shades, and a to-die-for light fixture.

CLOCKWISE, FROM ABOVE: This large abstract painting by Julia Contacessi felt almost like it was made for this room both in scale and palette. I Spindle-style wood sconces pop off the navy grass cloth and offer a nod to this home's coastal location. I A wood side table adds warmth and texture, while a custom-made zebra x-bench fits snugly between the two built-in bookcases, offering up another place to perch.

OPPOSITE: The two-tone paint treatment in this office by Kate Coughlin is a great alternative to standard white trim. The pops of orange are a perfect contrast to all the blue.

LEFT: I like to find accessories that really stand out on a dark built-in, as Kate Coughlin did here in this space she designed.

USE ALL SURFACES

One of our favorite ways to stay organized at our office is pinboards and memo boards. We had some HUGE custom pinboards made for our walls in fabric and trim that coordinated with our space (check Etsy to find a vendor of your own). Having storage and display space on the walls as well as desks and drawers is hugely helpful in a creative field or when you are a busy mom trying to keep a grasp on everyone's schedule.

DOUBLE DUTY

Many times home offices share space with other rooms, most often a guest room or den. My best advice? Get a luxurious sleeper sofa that is comfy both for watching a movie AND for sleeping on and looks appropriate in scale with the rest of the furniture in the room. Alternatively, daybeds with a trundle are a great option as they can sleep a guest or two and act as a sofa within an office or den space. If your office does double duty, it's also really important to have an easy way to clean up and make the space look presentable—built-ins and bookshelves with bins or baskets are our favorite ways to accomplish this.

ABOVE, LEFT: In photographer Sarah Winchester's den, the room and trim were painted Farrow & Ball's Black Blue, highlighting the original fireplace and camouflaging the television.

ABOVE, RIGHT: Sarah Winchester's cat Magnolia finds a peaceful seat atop her daughter's miniature leopard chair.

OPPOSITE: In this warm and welcoming den by Alison Sheffield, old and new collide in front of an original wood-burning fireplace.

LEFT: Jenn Feldman designed this cozy banquette complete with shelf storage underneath. Welcoming even to pets!

CREATE DRAMA

Use a dark paint color or have window treatments made out of a favorite patterned fabric. This room is a bonus and therefore I give you permission to go a little crazy. A space that feels "you" and is filled with your favorite colors, patterns, and items will inspire you to work or relax, whichever you need to do more of in your life. A sad, ignored space won't help with either, so be sure to give this space attention and do something a little over the top or special in it.

DON'T TAKE IT TOO SERIOUSLY

Life can be crazy, and with kids it can sometimes be flat-out insane. Your once perfectly neat home can turn into a disaster zone worthy of FEMA in a matter of minutes. But if approached with thoughtfulness, careful consideration, and an attitude of joy, it can be a space that everyone in the family can appreciate. A place for the kids to be loud and spill Legos, a place where you can all snuggle together and watch *Toy Story* for the eight hundredth time, and a place where you can close the door and be alone in peace and quiet (with wine), if only for a few moments. When everyone has a space they can claim as theirs, the home is a respite from the world and a place where everyone can feel understood, cared for, and happy. I hope this book has helped you feel empowered to be brave, thoughtful, creative, bold, and, most importantly, inspired to keep trying again and again when things don't turn out as you hoped. There is no perfect home, no perfect parent, no perfect job . . . but there is beauty in the imperfections if you look hard enough.

ACKNOWLEDGMENTS

It's so much harder to write a book when you are a working parent, so hats off to my patient and thoughtful editor Trish Todd at Atria Books for gracefully fielding my deadline-delay requests and having faith in me that I would eventually finish this book. I'm still amazed I did.

Equally patient and positive was my agent, Brettne Bloom, who is the BEST cheerleader in the business.

In no way is this a one-woman show, so a BIG, HUGE thank-you to the Erin Gates Design team for helping me get this done, talk me off cliffs, do everything in their power to execute my design dreams, and listen to Baxter and Oliver bark their heads off every day. Allison, Lindsey, Katie, Molly, Eliza, and Melissa, you prop me up and make me look way better than I am.

I am lucky to end up calling most of my clients friends, and I thank them for not only trusting me to design their homes but then letting me photograph them and show them off. I'm always humbled when someone allows me into their lives in this way.

To my blog readers, many who have been following me on this journey for the past decade, THANK YOU. Your support, comments, and interest in what I do are nothing short of amazing. I am in debt to you all for this mind-blowing career I have, because without you, none of this would be.

This book is a bit different from the last in that I featured spaces done by other designers. I feel that as an industry we are only great when we support one another and inspire each other with our ideas. So thank you to them for generously sharing their work with me.

To my photographers, Michael J. Lee and Sarah Winchester, thank you for making my work look its very best (and sometimes even better than it is!). Your talent and eye are crucial to making my job successful, so thanks for waiting around while I find the perfect vase to put those flowers in.

Becoming a parent gives you incredible insight into what a pain in the butt you were to raise, so thanks to Mom and Dad for changing my diapers, paying for college, and letting me live past the age of fifteen. Bravo.

A big thank-you to Danege, the woman who lets me go to work without a worry in the world about the safety and care of my child. Our badass nanny can rock a mohawk AND make sure Henry remembers his please's and thank-you's.

ANDREW GATES!

My Henry. You are the essence of my being and everything I ever dreamed of. I love you more than you will ever know. But I will try my best to make sure you have some clue.

DESIGN RESOURCE GUIDE

A comprehensive list of my favorite spots to shop for clients (and myself!).
* Indicates a to-the-trade-only resource

LIGHTING

Circa Lighting
circalighting.com

Rejuvenation
rejuvenation.com

Hudson Valley Lighting
hudsonvalleylighting.com

Schoolhouse
schoolhouse.com

Currey & Company
curreycodealers.com

Dunes and Duchess
dunesandduchess.com

Robert Abbey
robertabbey.biz

Oomph
oomphhome.com

Coleen & Company
coleenandcompany.com

The Urban Electric Co.*
urbanelectricco.com

Vaughan*
vaughandesigns.com

Arteriors
arteriorshome.com

Ro Sham Beaux
ro-sham-beaux.com

Candelabra
shopcandelabra.com

Shades of Light
shadesoflight.com

FURNITURE

Mitchell Gold +
Bob Willams
mgbwhome.com

Roger + Chris
rogerandchris.com

CR Laine
crlaine.com

Kravet*
kravet.com

Century Furniture
centuryfurniture.com

Jonathan Adler
jonathanadler.com

Bernhardt Furniture
Company*
bernhardt.com

Ethan Allen
ethanallen.com

Wisteria
wisteria.com

Oly Studio*
olystudio.com

Ballard Designs
ballarddesigns.com

Redford House
redfordhouse.com

The CEH
theceh.com

Room & Board
roomandboard.com

Serena & Lily
serenaandlily.com

Made Goods
madegoods.com

Duralee*
duralee.com

Bungalow 5
bungalow5.com

DwellStudio
dwellstudio.com

Björk Studio
bjorkstudio.com

Kristin Drohan Collection
kristindrohancollection.
com

livenUPdesign
etsy.com/shop/
livenUPdesign

Lee Industries*
leeindustries.com

The New Traditionalists
thenewtraditionalists.com

Anthropologie
anthropologie.com

Lillian August
lillianaugust.com

Hickory Chair*
hickorychair.com

Crate and Barrel
crateandbarrel.com

Palecek*
palecek.com

TEXTILES & WALLCOVERINGS

Farrow & Ball
us.farrow-ball.com

Schumacher
fschumacher.com

Sister Parish Design
sisterparishdesign.com

Katie Ridder
katieridder.com

Peter Dunham Textiles
peterdunhamtextiles.com

Duralee
duralee.com

Kravet
kravet.com

Quadrille
quadrillefabrics.com

Colefax and Fowler
cowtan.com/colefax-and
-fowler

Pierre Frey
pierrefrey.com

Rogers & Goffigon
rogersandgoffigon.com

Hygge & West
hyggeandwest.com

Phillip Jeffries
phillipjeffries.com

Jane Shelton
janeshelton.com

Brunschwig & Fils
kravet.com/brunschwig-
fils

Les Indiennes
lesindiennes.com

Jasper by Michael Smith
michaelsmithinc.com

Ralph Lauren
ralphlauren.com/home

Raoul Textiles
raoultextiles.com/home

Christopher Farr
christopherfarr.com

Galbraith & Paul
galbraithandpaul.com

Osborne & Little
osborneandlittle.com

Spoonflower
spoonflower.com

ACCESSORIES

Jayson Home
jaysonhome.com

Wisteria
wisteria.com

Ballard Designs
ballarddesigns.com

Pottery Barn
potterybarn.com

West Elm
westelm.com

High Street Market
highstreetmarket.com

Terrain
shopterrain.com

Etsy
etsy.com

McGee & Co.
mcgeeandco.com

Target
target.com

HomeGoods
homegoods.com

Pigeon & Poodle
pigeonandpoodle.com

Williams Sonoma Home
williams-sonoma.com

One Kings Lane
onekingslane.com

ARTWORK

Elizabeth Mayville
emayville.com

Leslee Mitchell Art
lesleemitchellart.com

Etsy
etsy.com

Jules Place
julesplace.com

Amanda Stone Talley
amandatalley.com

Mallory Page
mallorypage.com

Wendover Art Group*
wendoverart.com

Minted
minted.com

Artfully Walls
artfullywalls.com

Gregg Irby Gallery
greggirbygallery.com

Susan Calloway Fine Arts
callowayart.com

Anne Irwin Fine Art
anneirwinfineart.com

Chase Young Gallery
chaseyounggallery.com

Michael Gaillard
Photography
michaelgaillard.com

Christina Baker
christinabaker.net

Kayce Hughes
kaycehughes.com

Panteek
panteek.com

One Kings Lane
onekingslane.com

KIDS' FURNITURE & DÉCOR

Pottery Barn Kids
potterybarnkids.com

PBteen
pbteen.com

Ducduc
ducducnyc.com

West Elm
westelm.com

Serena & Lily
serenaandlily.com

Biscuit
biscuit-home.com

Room & Board
roomandboard.com

RH Baby & Child
rhbabyandchild.com

Crate and Kids
crateandbarrel.com/kids

Rosenberry Rooms
rosenberryrooms.com

The Beautiful Bed
Company
beautifulbedco.com

Roller Rabbit
rollerrabbit.com

PAINT

Behr
behr.com

Benjamin Moore
benjaminmoore.com

Clark & Kensington
thepaintstudio.com

Farrow & Ball
us.farrow-ball.com

Sherwin-Williams
sherwin-williams.com

Valspar
valsparpaint.com

HARDWARE

Schoolhouse Electric
schoolhouse.com

Rejuvenation
rejuvenation.com

Top Knobs Décor
topknobsdecor.com

Nest Studio
neststudiocollection.com

Classic Brass
classic-brass.com

Restoration Hardware
restorationhardware.com

Home Depot
homedepot.com

Emtek
emtek.com

RUGS

Stark Carpet
starkcarpet.com

Landry & Arcari
landryandarcari.com

Old New House
oldnewhouse.com

Dash & Albert
annieselke.com/c/
dashandalbert

Etsy
etsy.com

Elizabeth Eakins
elizabetheakins.com

Restoration Hardware
restorationhardware.com

Momeni
momeni.com

Horchow
horchow.com

Williams Sonoma Home
williams-sonoma.com

MWI Fiber-Shield
mwifibershield.com

BEDDING

Matouk
matouk.com

Leontine Linens
leontinelinens.com

Julia B.
juliab.com

Biscuit Bedding
biscuit-home.com

Annie Selke
annieselke.com

Pottery Barn
potterybarn.com

Williams Sonoma Home
williams-sonoma.com

Restoration Hardware
restorationhardware.com

IMAGE CREDITS

PHOTOGRAPHY CREDITS

Allison, Brooke—page 136

Bartlam, Amy—pages 39, 93, 107, 111, 134, 135, 151, 156, 194, 226, 252, 267, 294

Barzin, Anna Routh—page 201

Butler, Emily—page 149

Cohen, Nicole—pages 50, 137, 293, 320

Delaney, Jessica—pages 94, 95

Ellis, Will, for Emily Gilbert—pages 195, 199

Ford, Maureen—pages v, 349

Gilbert, Emily—pages 52, 53, 54, 130, 142, 164, 168, 198, 271, 274, 314, 315

Gates, Erin—pages 41, 74

Grapevine Interiors—pages 172, 199

Grimm, Michael—pages 102, 253, 292

Gruen, John—page 153

Lee, Michael J.—cover, ii, vi, viii, xi, 3, 8, 10, 11, 14, 16, 17, 20, 22, 25, 26, 30, 32, 35, 38, 44, 46, 48, 49, 50, 56, 60, 62, 63, 64, 65, 66, 67, 68, 69, 75, 76, 78, 90, 96, 100, 101, 105, 108, 109, 110, 128, 129, 143, 144, 146, 147, 148, 150, 151, 153, 158, 159, 162, 165, 169, 173, 174, 175, 176, 177, 178, 179, 184, 185, 186, 195, 196, 198, 209, 210, 211, 214, 216, 217, 218, 220, 221, 223, 228, 229, 232, 233, 234, 236, 237, 238, 239, 246, 247, 248, 249, 250, 251, 252, 253, 254, 256, 257, 258, 259, 262, 263, 264, 265, 269, 270, 272, 275, 276, 277, 278, 280, 281, 284, 286, 287, 289, 291, 294, 296, 298, 299, 301, 302, 303, 304, 306, 307, 310, 312, 313, 316, 317, 321, 322, 323, 328, 329, 330, 332, 334, 335, 336, 337, 346, 350, 356

Litchfield, Sean—pages 110, 235

Lorenz, Megan—pages 70, 157, 202, 279

Marengo, Staci—pages 166, 167

Millet, Karyn R.—page 347

Moss, Marissa—page 166

Nantucket Architectural Photography—page 92

Tubridy, Sean—page 212

Winchester, Sarah M.—12, 28, 30, 36, 37, 40, 42, 43, 51, 58, 59, 64, 72, 73, 79, 82, 83, 84, 85, 86, 87, 88, 89, 97, 98, 104, 106, 117, 118, 119, 120, 121, 122, 123, 124, 126, 127, 132, 133, 137, 138, 140, 141, 144, 145, 149, 160, 161, 163, 165, 168, 170, 173, 180, 182, 183, 188, 189, 190, 191, 192, 193, 195, 200, 201, 202, 224, 225, 226, 227, 230, 231, 240, 241, 242, 243, 244, 245, 260, 261, 266, 268, 274, 276, 279, 282, 283, 285, 286, 288, 290, 291, 295, 299, 300, 305, 319, 323, 324, 325, 326, 327, 338, 339, 340, 341, 342, 343, 344, 355

INTERIOR DESIGN CREDITS

Anna Burke Interiors—page 164

Anna Matthews Interiors—page 201

Butler, Emily—pages 50, 137, 149, 293, 320

Coughlin, Kate—pages 42, 43, 137, 163, 202, 260, 295, 342, 343

Dalrymple, Nikki, for Acquire Interior Design—pages 110, 235

Gates, Erin—cover, ii, vi, viii, xi, 3, 8, 10, 11, 12, 14, 16, 17, 20, 22, 25, 26, 28, 30, 32, 35, 36, 37, 38, 40, 44, 46, 48, 49, 50, 51, 56, 58, 59, 60, 62, 63, 64, 66, 67, 68, 69, 74, 75, 76, 78, 82, 83, 84, 85, 86, 87, 88, 89, 90, 96, 100, 101, 104, 105, 106, 108, 109, 110, 117, 118, 119, 120, 121, 122, 123, 124, 126, 127, 128, 129, 132, 133, 138, 140, 141, 143, 144, 145, 146, 147, 148, 150, 151, 153, 158, 159, 160, 161, 162, 165, 169, 170, 173, 174, 175, 176, 177, 178, 179, 180, 182, 183, 184, 185, 186, 195, 196, 200, 209, 210, 211, 214, 216, 217, 218, 220, 221, 223, 226, 227, 228, 229, 230, 231, 232, 233, 234, 236, 237, 238, 239, 244, 245, 248, 249, 250, 251, 252, 254, 256, 257, 258, 259, 261, 262, 263, 264, 265, 266, 268, 269, 270, 272, 274, 275, 276, 277, 278, 279, 280, 281, 284, 285, 286, 287, 288, 289, 290, 291, 294, 296, 298, 299, 300, 301, 302, 303, 304, 305, 306, 307, 310, 312, 313, 316, 317, 319, 321, 321, 322, 323, 324, 325, 326, 327, 328, 329, 330, 332, 334, 335, 336, 337, 339, 340, 341, 350, 355

Garelick, Ashley—pages 224, 225

Grapevine Interiors—pages 172, 198, 199

Feldman, Jenn—pages 39, 93, 107, 111, 134, 135, 151, 156, 194, 226, 252, 267, 294, 347

Ferraro, Dana, for Molly Patton Design—page 136

Hanson, Lindsey—pages 84–86, 138, 140, 141

Henry, Robin—page 168

Hether, Darci—page 195

Hirsch, Nicole—pages 188–191

Holland, Dina—pages 94, 95

KidderKokx Interior Architecture & Design—pages 240, 241, 282, 283

Knox, Patricia—pages 92, 102, 253, 292

Lovejoy Interiors—page 153

Miller, Jessie D.—pages 70, 157, 202, 279

Reynolds, Nicole—page 166

Richard, Julie—pages 64, 168, 201, 268, 338

Scales, Sarah—pages 72, 73, 98, 192, 193

Sheffield, Alison—pages 65, 246, 247, 253, 291, 346

Simonds, Colleen—pages 52, 53, 54, 130, 142, 271, 274, 314, 315

Sklar, Amy—pages 166, 167

TBHCo—pages 198, 199

Walker, Cecilia—pages 165, 173, 195

Winchester, Sarah M.—pages 79, 97, 149, 242, 243, 276, 279, 344, 355

ARTWORK

Adams, Lauren—pages 82, 238

Baker, Christina—pages 120, 140

Bartley, Mary Ellen—pages 310, 313

Blakeney, Kristen—page 218

Breidenbach, Shelli—page 239

Cohen, Nicole—page 157

Contacessi, Julia—page 341

Duncan, Tiel—page 159

Gaillard, Michael—page 275

Goldsmith, Scott—page 314

ILLUSTRATION CREDITS

Monogram Guide, page 318:

Larsen McDowell for Cece DuPraz

SPECIAL IMAGE CREDITS

Book Spine

Chinoiserie Toile—Willow Ware Blue & White by Sarah Mason Walden for Peacoquette Designs

Paint Samples, pages 112–113, 204–205, 222:

Sarah M. Winchester

Stylish Sectionals, pages 18–19:

Classic & Cozy: Mitchell Gold + Bob Williams Keaton Sectional

Tight Back & Tufted: Roger + Chris Atticus Sectional

Tailored Slipcover: Kravet Inc. Roland Sofa by Thom Filicia

Streamlined Base: Mitchell Gold + Bob Williams Clifton Sectional

Traditional Roll Arm: Roger + Chris Blythe Sectional

Chesterfield: Century Furniture Modern Chesterfield Sofa

Modern Bench Seat: CR Laine Taylor Sectional

Contemporary: Jonathan Adler Danner Sectional

Pairing Off, pages 80–81:

Circa Lighting Hicks Large Pendant

Circa Lighting Darlana Linear Lantern

Hudson Valley Lighting Pelham Pendant

Hudson Valley Lighting weeny Chandelier

Rejuvenation Hood Classic Globe

Circa Lighting Classic Ring Chandelier

Rejuvenation Rose City 4" Pendant

Circa Lighting Venetian Medium Chandelier

Circa Lighting Agnes Small Pendant

Circa Lighting Bistro Four Arm Chandelier

Circa Lighting Darlana Small Lantern

Circa Lighting Caron Large Chandelier

Circa Lighting Goodman Small Hanging Light

Circa Lighting Paris Flea Market Large Chandelier

Baby to Big Kid, pages 154–155:

Art:

Leslee Mitchell Art, Car Series Red, 75

Elizabeth Mayville, Top Knot 24

Wallpaper:

Sister Parish, Serendipity Wallcovering

Farrow & Ball, Closet Stripe

Chinois Palais in Blush Conch from the Mary McDonald II Collection from Schumacher

Furniture:

Bungalow 5, Isabella Dresser

DwellStudio, Loren End Table

Bed:

PBteen, Elsie Daybed & Trundle

Serena & Lily, Harbour Cane Bed

Fabrics:

Peter Dunham Textiles, Kashmir Paisley

Katie Ridder, Peony in Blueberry

Duralee, Quintessence, Tilton Fenwick Collection

Storage:

Pottery Barn Kids, Charlie Writing Desk & Hutch

Jonathan Adler, Jacques Etagère

A Nonmatchy Master, pages 308–309:

Bernhardt Furniture, Auberge Poster Bed

Bernhardt Furniture, Auberge Chest

Bernhardt Furniture, Cabrillo Nailhead Dresser

Mitchell Gold + Bob Williams Regis Tall King Bed

Jonathan Adler, Channing End Table

Jonathan Adler, Channing Dresser

Ethan Allen, Quincy Bed

The CEH, Jillian Side Table

Serena & Lily, Blake Raffia Wide Dresser

Jonathan Adler, Lampert Headboard

Duralee, Windsor Side Table

Made Goods, Lindsey Dresser

Orly Studio, Macro Bed

Redford House, Bennett Nightstand

Room & Board, Berkeley Dresser

Wisteria, Mestre Ivory Linen Headboard

Ballard Designs, Kendall Side Table

Redford House, Swedish Dresser

CHAPTER OPENER IMAGES

Family Spaces: Lee Jofa, Allegra in Blues

Kid Spaces: Brunschwig & Fils, Onam Paisley in Indigo

Parent Retreats: Kravet Couture, Bambu Fret in Ciel by Jan Showers Designs

Endpapers: Brunschwig & Fils, Le Zebre in Beige

The back cover: Kravet, Lodi in Sail by Thom Filicia

ERIN T. GATES is an interior designer, blogger, and author of the *New York Times* bestselling *Elements of Style: Designing a Home & a Life*. She has been featured in various publications such as *O, the Oprah Magazine, Redbook, Better Homes & Gardens, Elle Decor, House & Home,* the *Boston Globe,* and the *Wall Street Journal.* She lives outside of Boston with her husband and son.